# BLIND
# SPOT

# IT

OLIVE
PRESS

# BLIND SPOT

## A LEADER'S GUIDE TO IT-ENABLED BUSINESS TRANSFORMATION

CHARLIE FELD

This book is dedicated to my wife, Cindy, and sons, Jon and Kenny, who supported my journey through "40 Years of Hard Road" and to my nephew, Brad, who invested time, energy, and money to help scale The Feld Group.

# TABLE OF CONTENTS

# FOREWORD

## By Herb Kelleher
## Founder and Chairman Emeritus, Southwest Airlines

Let me start out by saying I am not the foremost fan of computers, e-mails, blogging, tweeting or anything that makes contact between people detached and perhaps somewhat sterile. You learn more looking into a Customer's or an Employee's eyes than you can ever learn from an e-mail. To me, computers should always be servants; never masters.

When it comes to corporate IT, I understood why the accountants need computers to close the books but no one ever showed me the value inclusive IT can bring to things that matter to Customers — like on-time arrivals, ease of boarding or ability to respond to a weather delay — until I met Charlie Feld in 2002.

Charlie has a way of connecting with non-IT leaders that makes a complex topic like IT simple to grasp. Many IT people seem to enjoy taking a complex idea and making it more complex or sometimes they say you're going to have to give up your business plan and impair your Customer Service in order to accommodate the technology. Charlie said, to the contrary, the purpose of IT is to promote your business plan and enhance your Customer Service. The interesting part of the framework you will read about in this book was that we were spending enough money on Technology but not getting full, tangible value because we simply weren't managing it right.

Having said that, I still don't think a good manager or leader should hide behind his/her computer. Nothing will ever replace being with Customers and Employees. The IT goal should be to enable you to do more of that because your operation can run more smoothly and get you out of crisis management. This is an important topic and an easy book to read. You should be able to scan it on a Southwest Airlines flight between Dallas and Chicago.

# PREFACE

## 40 Years of Hard Road
### *Lessons Learned, Lessons Shared*

My journey started in 1966 when IBM hired me to become a systems engineer. I had never seen a computer before and did not know what a systems engineer did. However, the job paid well and sounded more important than selling IBM typewriters. It has turned out to be a wonderful journey for me. At the time, who would have conceived of Google, or buying books on Amazon and songs on iTunes, or even ATMs instead of bank tellers? All of these technologies were created and matured during the course of my 40-year career.

What has not matured during that same explosive period is the management framework that would enable the efficient application of these rich technologies within large enterprises. Every decade, more enterprises are assimilating information technology (IT), business processes, and human assets into a more-modern model. But the potential of IT still far exceeds the ability of most organizations, industries, and governments to harness it.

I was fortunate that, after building a strong knowledge base and competence for 15 years at IBM, I became the head of IT at Frito-Lay, a division of PepsiCo. It was there that my team and I had a very successful early implementation of a business transformation using mobile technology for the frontline sales force—tying it to all of Frito-Lay's backend manufacturing, distribution, purchasing, and financial systems. The management framework that I describe in this book had its origin at Frito-Lay during the 1980s. It is extremely simple and easy to understand.

After over a decade, I left Frito-Lay and PepsiCo—not out of boredom or frustration, the usual reasons for moving on, but out of a spirit of adventure and experimentation. I really wondered if the awards we had won at Frito-Lay from the Smithsonian Institute and Carnegie Mellon University were lucky, one-time events or indicative of a broader concept. I wanted to see if I could apply my management framework in another company and industry—with an entirely different executive team and IT organization—and achieve similar results. I was confident, but not sure, that I could replicate another large-scale transformation.

In 1992, I started The Feld Group along with two of my leaders from Frito-Lay, Monte Jones and Pat Steele. The business idea was not to consult with IT organizations, but to be hired by CEOs to run their IT groups under contract. The first Feld Group client was Jerry Grinstein at the Burlington Northern Railroad. Since we had no rail industry experience, we went to the CSX Railroad and recruited our first team, which became known as the "Jacksonville 5" since that was where they all lived. Stan Alexander became our CTO and Keith Halbert led the customer support systems. The rest we recruited directly into Burlington Northern.

As you will read later in this book, we made great progress and further proved that having this framework allowed us to measure our progress, correct course where necessary, and most important, communicate complex issues in simple ways—both internally within the IT department and externally with the business leadership, customers, board of directors, and Wall Street.

In 1994, I got a call from Mike Jordan, my former boss at Frito-Lay, who had retired from PepsiCo and was now Chairman and CEO of Westinghouse in Pittsburgh. Since Mike and I had worked together along with his CFO, Fred Reynolds, and his Chief Personnel Officer, Dave Zemelman—all formerly at PepsiCo—he wanted to hire The Feld Group.

The problem was my full-time involvement at Burlington Northern. However, I was so confident in our approach—one that was getting richer by the year—that I offered to hire and train a Feld Group team for him and oversee the work. To fill that gap we hired two young IBMers, Mike Koehler and Bruce Graham, and dispatched them to Pittsburgh with Monte Jones forming our second team.

It was really exciting for me to watch as the framework was extended and enriched beyond me. That team spent the next couple of years helping to transform a struggling Westinghouse into a vibrant CBS media company through restructuring, asset sales, acquisitions, and consolidation.

From there we began to add more teams and solidify the management system with companies like WellPoint, Coca-Cola, Delta Air Lines, Kemper Insurance, Coors, Southwest Airlines, Payless Shoes, The Home Depot, First Data Resources, and many others. In some, we ran the full operating model, and in others —like FedEx—we provided a structured consulting engagement. We operated The Feld Group for twelve years (1992–2004). During those twelve years we successfully solidified our framework, proved that it was repeatable, and significantly improved the odds of success for big IT-enabled business transformations. More important, it was no longer about only me being able to be successful. The Feld Group had become a company full of successful IT leaders building on each other's successes and sharing a common way of leading IT. EDS acquired us in 2004—not for our consulting business, but for our 50-person leadership team.

In 2008, Hewlett Packard bought EDS, and I took my retirement. Over the last year, I have rekindled my passion for this young profession that has brought me so much. I am now focused on moving this approach to managing this critical capability into its next phase. By making this framework available beyond just myself and my former Feld Group colleagues, I hope that it can be adopted by many otherwise competent business and IT executives and used to advance their 21st century agendas.

This approach, more than anything else, can begin to demystify information technology and eliminate it as a blind spot or stumbling block for business leaders. I would consider it a great legacy and contribution to the profession if just a few organizations gain new insight by embracing the framework in this book.

# INTRODUCTION

A blind spot can be described as a subject that is obscure or unintelligible to otherwise sharp and intelligent people. Information technology (IT), unfortunately, is that kind of subject to many business leaders. I say "unfortunately" because IT can either enable or disable an enterprise to sustain vibrancy and success in the 21st century.

This is becoming more apparent every year, particularly to those successful, large, 20th century enterprises in which IT has become an expensive inhibitor of the speed and agility required for competing in a global, supply-chain-driven, customer-centric economy.

## An Introduction to the Framework

This book describes a framework that I have developed and improved over the last 30 years with a variety of organizations, including Frito-Lay, Burlington Northern Santa Fe, Delta Air Lines, Home Depot, and Southwest Airlines. This framework (diagrammed in Figure 1, and discussed in detail in Chapter 2) consists of four planks that form a platform for change and five phases that pace the execution over several years. Together they create a journey. The beauty of this framework is that it demystifies technology to the non-experts among us, is simple, and—like most principle-based approaches—is durable through the eras and across industries.

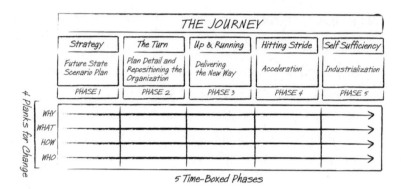

Figure 1

I positioned The Feld Group as an IT leadership, turnaround firm. We would come into an organization and do a 90-day strategy development around the four WHY, WHAT, HOW, and WHO planks for change:

WHY (Why do anything?)
WHAT (What will we do?)
HOW (How will we do it?)
WHO (Who will lead and manage the change?)

If the strategy was compelling and the executive team was willing to make the required changes, then we would contract to actually run the IT organization for two years. I would join the executive team under contract, and not as an employee.

As part of the first 90 days, we would articulate a future state plan and assess the skills, structures, and leadership abilities within the technology group. We would then fill the top-25 IT-leadership positions with as many of the existing players as possible and bring the rest in—either from The Feld Group or by recruiting directly into our client's enterprise. We would proceed during the first year in a very structured way from the Strategy, to The Turn, to Up and Running in 90-day increments. By the second year we would be Hitting Stride while delivering real change and value to the organization. At the end of the second year, we would find our replacements and transition out. The goal was to leave the organization stronger and Self-Sufficient.

I will turn to this framework throughout the book, so consider bookmarking Figure 1 for quick reference.

Although the complete journey to business transformation requires both the four planks for change and the five time-boxed phases, this book is specifically focused on what the executive team needs to do to develop a change agenda: creating the four planks for change. The book defines and describes the principles and mechanisms that give the WHY, the WHAT, and the HOW motion and meaning for your enterprise. However, real results and execution will always boil down to the people and the leadership culture. That is the WHO.

The focus is on business leadership and creating a dialogue with the IT organization. If you get the right leadership team in place, hire the right people, pick the right partners, and manage to a consistent framework, then this systems capability can quickly be turned from a liability to an asset in any organization.

The backbone of this book is the story of my own experience developing and then applying the framework when I was CIO at Frito-Lay during the 1980s. In a series of chapters that serve as brief introductions to the framework, I show how we moved through the WHY, WHAT, HOW, and WHO at Frito-Lay as we first realized the need to change, and then developed and implemented a revolutionary IT-enabled solution for our sales team that transformed the company—and the industry.

I'll also use Frito-Lay to describe the journey from our then-current-state business/IT model in 1984 to our future state in 1988. This journey required us to make massive changes throughout the organization while running a high-transaction, multi-billion-dollar business.[1]

## *Frito-Lay Journey*

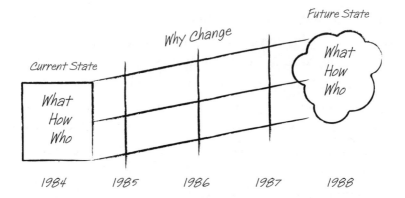

To reinforce the components of the framework, I'll use examples of specific corporations we worked with that have made significant transformational progress to a more-modern 21st-century enterprise. Some are very far along, while others have just recently begun. Each has followed this framework and all have developed an excellent dialogue between the business and IT leadership.

I'll use Home Depot to illustrate WHY organizations hit a point where their old and successful model needs to change.

Burlington Northern Santa Fe Railroad is a good example of the WHAT. I will consider what we set out to achieve in their business architecture, why was it compelling, how was it articulated to the business leaders and the board of directors, and what role IT played in enabling the business model.

[1]Harvard Business School Case Study Frito-Lay Inc.: A Strategic Transition (Consolidated) July, 1993

Southwest Airlines will be my core example of the HOW. I'll explore how to implement modern design and technologies, how projects and programs need to be managed, the connective tissue between the business architecture, the applications architecture and the technical architecture, and how technology choices are made and adhered to in an ever-changing landscape. In short, the principles of world-class IT execution that non-IT leaders can comprehend.

I will return to Frito-Lay and PepsiCo to describe the WHO. The leadership and organizational component of the framework is, I believe, the foundation for success. Putting the right people in the right structure—whether insourced or outsourced—is the key to execution of the WHAT and the HOW. High-performance teams and collaboration within the IT organization and between IT and their business partners is critical. In addition, the role of the executive committee in governance, business accountability and decision rights, and corporate culture are all ingredients in successful and sustainable execution.

I did not write this book nor design this framework to convince anyone to invest in IT. Instead, I wrote this book to improve your odds of success and reduce risk once you have decided for yourself that IT matters.

This is, however, where we encounter the dilemma of the blind spot. Most senior leaders have learned enough about the workings of their businesses to feel comfortable engaging in a new-product dialogue or a complex financial debate or a major litigation. But few have adequate background to understand and lead wide-scale changes that are technology enabled. They have developed enough of a foundation in most functional areas to be able to probe, push, form a point of view, and make informed decisions. However, when faced with discussions and decisions in the area of information technology, their eyes quickly glaze over and they hope their IT organizations or consultants get it right. To most executives, IT is a blind spot—a discipline that is confusing and hard to understand.

My belief is that information technology should not be viewed as a complex functional area. It is an integrating discipline that enables the other functions to operate as a seamless, well-run business. Instead of some mysterious black box, IT can be less complex and easier to understand than marketing, operations, finance, sales, and other traditional operational disciplines. This is because it is fundamentally all about the way a business should operate, manifested in information access, workflows, networks, and business rules. And instead of a blind spot, information technology can and should be a highly visible and well-understood part of every business leader's knowledge base.

To be successful in the next decade, executives will be required to develop a reasonable foundation for using systems and technology to transform their organizations—to confidently enter the dialogue, avoid the fads of the moment, and embrace their role in shaping and integrating their corporations' technological initiatives. Modern enterprises will seamlessly integrate technology into the way they do business—and if they have not already begun this journey, they will need to do so as soon as possible. This journey will be a multiyear, pervasive effort that will require executive leadership if it is to be fully successful.

It may seem that there is no good time to make big changes like this. When times are good you can afford the necessary changes, but the WHY feels weak. That switches 180 degrees when you start having trouble. The impetus to start making big changes in the midst of turbulent times like these may seem counterintuitive. However, right now you have what may constitute a once-in-a-lifetime license to make dramatic change. The economic downturn has created a global referendum for change, and you hold the keys to change in your organization.

Think about WHAT is now possible.

You may have a unique opportunity to right-size your workforce and to build a leaner, flatter, and more agile organization; to restructure, reengineer, and rejuvenate your business; to tear out old and inefficient processes, facilities, and ways of doing business; to put in simpler, faster, and less-expensive systems; and to renegotiate contracts with your employees and your suppliers that will dramatically change your cost structure. You might have the opening to sell off underperforming plants and other assets, generating short-term cash while avoiding future drains on your resources. You can consider taking write-offs that you would have never contemplated taking a year or two ago, and get them off your books once and for all. Now you can simplify your business, even if it means making it temporarily smaller—but stronger, more flexible, and more competitive— and you can leverage modern technology to help enable your change agenda.

Ultimately, the goal of this book is to bring an executive team from a major enterprise together around this framework and to help them structure a dialogue about their future and the possibilities that IT can enable. It represents a unique model of like-minded operating people that I have worked with sharing an experience base, rather than suppliers or consultants advocating point solutions focused more on a particular project or a specific technology. It is built on a foundation of holistic results-oriented leadership, end-to-end management processes, and competitiveness.

After reading this book, not only will you understand how to apply this framework for organizational transformation, you'll understand how to pace the change as you go. With this understanding, you'll be able to reduce the risk of the journey to IT-enabled organizational transformation, while increasing the probability of success. And if there's a time that you cannot afford to fall behind in the transformation of your business, that time is now.

# CHAPTER 1

THE FRITO-LAY JOURNEY

## Driving IT-Enabled Business Transformation

# 1 THE FRITO-LAY JOURNEY
# Driving IT-Enabled Business Transformation

Frito-Lay was a special place in the 1980s, and the business change that occurred there was stunningly enabled by technology. It would be easier to tell the story of a business model change that was enabled by modern, leading-edge technology. But that would put more emphasis on the technology than on the business itself. In the early 1980s, the technology was so crude that it could not lead the business imagination.

Therefore, the WHY change and WHAT to change to were driven by competitiveness, serving customers, operational excellence, and a marketplace shift in the consumer-goods industry resulting from the effect of powerful Wal-Mart. My task, as the CIO at Frito-Lay, was to figure out HOW to get the job done and WHO to do it with. The case studies about the Frito-Lay transformation written by the Harvard Business School more than 20 years ago are still being taught today.

My belief is that many of the well-known, technology-enabled business-model changes had their roots in that era because that is when the choice between pure centralization or pure decentralization began to change. Frito-Lay had to figure out for itself a new kind of hybrid organization that has now become the ideal 21st-century model. This hybrid approach allowed certain functions to be centralized—and, therefore, highly leveraged—while other functions were operating at a unique level for each customer. We referred to it as "directed decentralization." The technology and business-process design is what enabled this new model to flourish and be both operationally excellent and innovative with customers.

Yet was it really a new model, or an old model on a larger scale that technology enabled?

In 1932, Herman Lay began a company in Nashville delivering snack foods to local businesses. In 1938, Lay bought the Atlanta-based manufacturer of the snack foods he was selling, changing the company's name to the H.W. Lay & Company in 1939. Corporate folklore had it that he bought the potatoes from the farmers, cooked them in his kitchens, sold them to his customers, and collected the money. I was blessed to spend time with him in the early 1980s when I became the CIO at Frito-Lay. He was in his 80s and retired, but still very active and vibrant.

I believe our sessions are what led me to be a better IT leader because he stressed the primacy of the business system rather than the technology.

Herman's main theme was that "no matter how big or complicated the company gets, we still just buy potatoes, cook them, put them in bags, sell them to our customers, and collect the money." He counseled me that although he did not know much about computers, he "reckoned" my job was to make it easy for people to do that. What a great and insightful learning moment for a new IT leader.

Over the years, Herman met Elmer Doolin, who founded the Frito Company in San Antonio, Texas, in 1932. By the late 1950s, each company had expanded separately, and—in 1961, two years after the death of Elmer Doolin—the companies joined forces, replicating the business model in 32 geographic areas with 46 plants covering the U.S.

The new Frito-Lay was a simple model of high-quality products that people liked to eat, stamped out by the millions with a successful cookie-cutter approach. Like most consumer-goods companies of that era, Frito-Lay was highly decentralized by region. Each region, in fact, was a semi-autonomous business. That format worked extremely well because the company's customers and competitors were also regional. For example, its grocery store customers A&P were concentrated in the Northeast, Ralph's was primarily on the West Coast, and Tom Thumb was in Texas. There were no national grocery chains such as Wal-Mart or Kroger's until years later.

Similarly, Frito-Lay's competitors were also regional in nature—companies like Utz, Wise, Better Made, and many more. However, the new Frito-Lay was the only one of the regional snack-food manufacturers that also had a national footprint.

In 1965, Herman Lay and Don Kendall of Pepsi-Cola decided to merge and form PepsiCo. Andy Pearson, a former McKinsey partner, became president of the new company. He was instrumental in launching the second era of Frito-Lay's legendary growth by driving the company to centralize and functionalize in order to gain leverage and economies of scale. Why compete with regional chip makers when Frito-Lay had a national footprint? Why not leverage purchasing, manufacturing, distribution, brand marketing, finance, and other operations?

Wayne Calloway, who eventually became chairman and CEO of PepsiCo, was the head of planning, and he was charged with helping the company reorganize and implement centralized planning and control systems. If that was the WHY and the WHAT of the 1960s and 1970s, the HOW was to leverage centralized mainframe computer systems. The first step was to roll up the regions into seven zones. I showed up at Frito-Lay in 1970 as an IBM systems engineer, responsible for helping Calloway and his team further centralize the company by consolidating the seven zones into one common set of systems at its Dallas, Texas headquarters.

The other challenge of the HOW dimension of this era was volume. The company was doubling its sales every four years at a 15–20 percent compounded annual rate. However, we were selling hundreds of millions of dollars of revenue in individual 25-to-50-cent bags. Our ability to keep up with the paperwork and keypunch volume would inevitably become a limiting factor to our long-term growth.

We first looked for a commercial solution, and we knew that optical character recognition (OCR) was the best bet at the time.

The technology was proven in a large, distributed sales force application—Avon had used it successfully for its thousands of sales representatives. However, we had several additional problems to solve that Avon did not. The first problem was that the number of line items—and, therefore, the number of characters per sale—were ten times higher than Avon's. The second problem was that our route salesmen worked standing up in a store or truck as opposed to having an indoor environment with a table to write on like the Avon representatives had.

The combination of these two particular problems made standard OCR products impractical. The probability that every sales ticket would be rejected by the system and then have to be worked on manually was quite high.

So we looked for a custom solution. We went to work with the IBM labs, which had invented a new digitizing technology used successfully in a banking application. The hope was that we could scan and accept the characters that traditional OCRs could recognize, and for those unrecognizable characters, the hardware would digitize and display them on a screen so that a human operator could correct them later at a computer terminal.

With that innovative solution implemented in the 1970s, we were able to support the business-driven need for growth and centralized systems.

I mention this story for two reasons. First, it is a perfect example of business-driven technology enablement. Too often I have seen the opposite—a technology solution looking for a business problem. Second, along with centralization, functionalization, operational excellence, outstanding R&D, and brand management, we continued to grow at double-digit rates, compounded annually. By 1978, the company was a billion-dollar cash machine for PepsiCo, and in 1982, annual revenues climbed to $2 billion.

In 1981, I left IBM and became the CIO for Frito-Lay. The phenomenal success of the company was fast becoming a huge technology challenge. It was forcing us to outgrow even the innovative OCR solution I had helped IBM bring to Frito-Lay. The sheer volume, growth, and line-item expansion—combined with aging, sun-setting technology—was driving my team and the sales leadership to look seriously for another solution. We began to prototype handheld mobile technology.

You can imagine how crude the devices were in the early '80s. Remember, this was the age of the TRS-80 desktop microcomputer from Radio Shack—with its whopping 4K of RAM—and IBM had not yet entered the personal computer (PC) business. The cost of handheld mobile technology was prohibitive at the time, quality and reliability were not industrial strength, and functionality was pitiful. And, to top it all off, the devices used more battery power than the truck in which they were intended to dock.

More important, we had very little support from the business. The need at the time was purely technology driven and not business driven. No matter how much I tried to describe the coming technological Armageddon, no one wanted to spend tens of millions of dollars solving what were considered to be my problems.

I realized then that the HOW alone will never drive change in an organization. The WHY and the WHAT must also be powerful and compelling. It was not until the business had a reason to change that I would get my OCR replacement. Since the business was still experiencing double-digit rates of revenue and profit growth, the company's executive team did not see any reason to change anything. (Life was good.)

But there was trouble on the horizon.

# CHAPTER 2

## The Framework

# 2 THE FRAMEWORK

In the Introduction I briefly described the framework that I have developed and improved over the last 30 years with a variety of organizations, including Frito-Lay, Burlington Northern Santa Fe, Delta Air Lines, Home Depot, and Southwest Airlines. This framework (detailed in Figure 1) comprises the four planks required to create a change platform or agenda for your enterprise, along with the five phases that pace the execution.

My focus in this book is on the first portion of the framework—the four planks—using examples from different companies, cultures, industries, and timeframes that I personally experienced. However, pacing and execution of the change agenda are of equal importance for real organizational change and impact, and they play a vital role in the overall journey to business transformation. It is for that reason that I describe the five time-boxed phases of the framework in more detail later in this chapter.

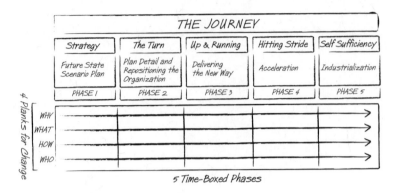

Figure 1

## The Four Planks

The primary focus of this book is on the first four planks of the change agenda developed during the Strategy phase. Developing the change agenda is the biggest and most important job of the executive team. It must be sturdy and durable enough to support the business as it undergoes the transformation process. The four planks of the change agenda are:

- The **WHY** change (WHY do anything?). This plank gives the platform durability. It more than anything else will enable the organization to mobilize, make investments, set priorities, take risks, and sustain the effort throughout the transformation. It is the business imperative that must be articulated by the executive team, or there is no point in launching a major transformation. Crafting the WHY is the responsibility of the executive leadership team (including the CIO) and it is described in detail in Chapter 3.

- The **WHAT** to change (WHAT will we do?). Assuming the WHY change is compelling and can be articulated, it becomes critical to describe what actually needs to change. It is equally important to describe what needs to stay the same. These conversations naturally gravitate toward centralization versus decentralization themes. A more appropriate dialogue should be focused on what gives you speed and customer centricity, and what gives you scale, leverage, and quality. This plank should fundamentally describe your future-state business model and be extremely agile. Chapter 4 goes into depth on the WHAT.

- The **HOW** to change (HOW will we do it?). This is the pathway from your current model to your future model, and it is where the heavy lifting comes in for both the business and the IT organization. To be successful, the following three principles within the HOW must be adhered to:

  HOW Principle I: Define and design a business, application, and technology blueprint and architecture before you begin investment and construction.

  HOW Principle II: Enforce a "Common Way" for development and quality engineering.

  HOW Principle III: Be disciplined in your approach to program and project management.

  I elaborate on the HOW—and these three principles—in Chapter 5.

- The **WHO** (WHO will lead and manage the change?) This is the last plank in the platform, and it is described in detail in Chapter 6. You will see my personal bias revealed in this chapter because, although I believe all of the planks are important, the human aspect makes the real difference! This chapter outlines the key human-resource principles required for sustained successes, including:

  WHO Principle I: Organization Matters
  WHO Principle II: Leadership Matters

WHO Principle III: Culture Matters

WHO Principle IV: Performance Matters

All of these human-resource principles matter whether you outsource, smartsource, or go it alone.

## The Five Time-Boxed Phases

The five time-boxed phases of the framework are where the business's executive and management team implement the organization's change agenda. Each phase has certain characteristics and outcomes that need to be constantly monitored and managed.

## Phase 1

In this phase—Strategy—the change agenda is fully articulated by the executive team, whose job it is to articulate a compelling WHY change, and a thoughtful future-state business model. One of the key pieces of work in this phase is to understand the gap between your current business model and the future state. This gap begins to define the work, timeframes, investments, and risks of the transformation. I refer to this as "scenario planning," and there are a number of different pathways that can be taken. The executive team needs to judge which scenario best fits the organization. This begins to shape the HOW and WHO portions of the agenda.

In almost every case, I have time-boxed this phase at between 90 and 120 days. That is enough time to shape and select the most appropriate scenario plan. The detail plan will then have shape and boundaries which can be further developed during the next phase—The Turn. Any longer than about 120 days, and the Strategy phase will become a "science fair" project. Any shorter than about 90 days, and it will not gain traction. This is mostly an executive committee-led effort, with heavy engagement by the systems leader/CIO.

## Phase 2

```
The Turn

Plan Detail and
Repositioning the
Organization

PHASE 2
```

The scenario plan gives meaning, direction, and pace to the transformation, and this should enable the business and IT organizations to drive a more detailed multi-year plan (MYP) for the Journey. Most of the work in this phase consists of sequencing and pacing the Journey from the current to future state. To do that in a quality way requires business and technology blueprints so that the construction process can be delivered in a series of releases that follow a clear roadmap.

The first release should also be articulated in The Turn and be broad enough to create a "beachhead" of visible success that is small enough to be built within the first year but large enough to be impactful. Full implementation can take longer. An example would be a modern gate-and-boarding system at Delta Air Lines.

The first release also serves to mobilize the organization change for leadership, structure, governance, and investment approach (WHO), and the "Common Way" quality engineering (HOW). This phase should be time-boxed for 90 days.

## Phase 3

This is a six-to-nine-month phase depending on the size and complexity of the Release 1 beachhead. The emphasis and burden switch from the WHY and WHAT, to the HOW and WHO. It also changes the primary work effort from the business leadership to the IT leadership. This phase is about quality construction, modern design and development, and IT capability building. The deal has been cut, and the blueprint, timeline, and investments are in place. Now it is about execution and delivering the new way. Leadership, culture, and performance all matter, and accountability is on the CIO and his/her team. That team may comprise of many partners, but make no mistake—the CIO is the general contractor.

## Phase 4

This is a Year 2 activity. The organization's course has been set in the Strategy, and The Turn and the New Way have been cultivated in the Up and Running. Now it is all about gaining speed, correcting course, and building organization muscle and confidence. But most of all, it is about quality delivery and productivity. The business team is also heavily engaged in deploying the Release 1 changes for business processes, metrics, incentives, culture, locations, and so forth.

## Phase 5

As the Journey enters Year 3, it is all about achieving consistency and quality delivery every six-to-nine months at a reasonable cost. Much of the burden shifts back to the business function to implement the IT-enabled changes and extract the value for the investment.

The framework is a combination of creating the change platform and phased execution. It helps create a solid journey for IT-enabled business transformation. In the chapters that follow, I will put my Frito-Lay experience into this end-to-end journey to describe how it works in the real world. Each chapter will show how we built the change agenda at Frito-Lay, highlighting each of the four planks (WHY, WHAT, HOW and WHO). I will then take a more generic look at how each of the four planks impacts your own business, followed by a case study showing the four planks in action.

# CHAPTER 3

WHY     WHAT     HOW     WHO
......

## THE WHY

# WHY Do Anything?

The WHY change (WHY do anything?). This plank gives the platform durability. It more than anything else will enable the organization to mobilize, make investments, set priorities, take risks, and sustain the effort throughout the transformation. It is the business imperative that must be articulated by the executive team, or there is no point in launching a major transformation. Crafting the WHY is the responsibility of the executive leadership team (including the CIO).

## 3A THE FRITO-LAY JOURNEY
# WHY We Made the Changes

By the early 1980s, Frito-Lay's double-digit revenue growth began to slow down. Sustaining double-digit growth on a multi-billion-dollar base is a difficult proposition in even the best market conditions. Our growth profile had been comprised of about five percent price inflation, five percent distribution growth, and five percent product innovation. As the '80s began, pricing became less of a weapon with the slowing of inflation and the entrance of a powerful Wal-Mart supply chain dynamic. Our route growth slowed as we had penetrated most every bit of real estate in the U.S. that had a grocery store, supermarket, or vending machine on it. As we used to like to say, "Stand on any corner for a few hours and you will see one of our 10,000 Frito-Lay trucks."

As revenue growth slowed, we had to lean more heavily on innovation and brand expansions to maintain profitability, which was still growing at double digits. At the same time, the cost side of the equation was very healthy as we continued to wring productivity improvements out of the system. The key factor behind our productivity growth was that throughout the 1970s and into the 1980s, we used our capital, R&D, and engineering to build high-tech mega plants and close the older, lower-tech, small regional facilities that were the foundation of the decentralized era. In addition, our distribution system of warehouses and long-haul and route trucks was constantly being re-engineered. The leverage and operational excellence were nothing short of stunning, and we were able to hold our profit growth to double digits even as revenue growth slowed to single digits.

However, we did recognize that this math was not sustainable into the 1990s. In fact, I vividly remember a hand-drawn graph on a flipchart produced by Mike Jordan in 1982. The graph showed that, at the current course and speed, the revenue and cost curves would cross in 1994—turning our money-making operation into a money-losing operation. That became our WHY change. However, while we all agreed intellectually that we needed to change, there were two obstacles blocking us from taking immediate action. The first obstacle was we did not know exactly WHAT to change. The second obstacle was there was no sense of urgency because we were still doing so well financially. The problem would not become grave for years—more than a decade into the future.

Like most people, countries, and companies, if the problem is seen to be in the distant future, then it is much harder to justify taking risks or making substantial changes in the near term. Consider, for example, if you are told by your doctor that you have some of the early warning signs of heart disease, such as high cholesterol, borderline high blood pressure, and a problematic genetic history. It would be difficult for anybody—with the exception of a very few highly disciplined people—to make the significant and lasting lifestyle changes required to turn around this outcome. Go forward ten years and have a stroke, however, and suddenly you'll do most anything you can to get your life back onto a healthy track. The real problem is that by then it may be too late.

The same is true for companies. All but a few will wait until the inevitable happens—and then it may be too late. Fortunately, PepsiCo in general, and Frito-Lay more specifically, will take action at the first sign of smoke, creating a "burning platform" that compels change. However, sometimes this sense of urgency or WHY can misfire because the WHAT is not thought through well enough.

Our burning platform change program was triggered by Bill Korn, the former head of sales and marketing, when he became Frito-Lay's CEO in 1984. However, although we knew the WHY change, we had not yet figured out the WHAT to change to. Bill came out of the Cola Wars and had a deep belief that market share was the key health indicator, not revenue growth nor profitability, and he was unwilling to give up even the smallest fraction of market share to anyone. This triggered a huge change program that refocused the company on where and to whom we were gaining or losing share—not just the national averages.

What this strategy pointed out was that our regional competitors were beginning to hammer us with regional preferences such as hard-bite potato chips in the Northeast, restaurant-style tortilla chips in the West, Cajun spice flavors in the Southeast, and so on. Bill concluded that this was truly a regional business—more like the original Herman Lay model—and not a national business.

With this determination, we had our WHY firmly in place.

## 3B

# WHY Do Anything?

Waves of innovation have had a transformational impact on the way work is done, where people live, how business is conducted, and how society has evolved. They have also had a huge impact on our nation's standard of living, our lifespan, our wealth, and our environment. These waves have accelerated in both number and velocity—particularly over the last half-century, as information, networks, and access have expanded to more nations, shrinking the world and creating a truly global new economic system.

In almost every decade since the mid-1800s, American inventors, engineers, and innovators have made their mark on this country—and on the world. The telephone and the phonograph were invented in the 1870s, photographic film and the AC motor in the 1880s, and radio in the 1890s. In the first decade of the

1900s, the Wright Brothers built and flew the first aircraft, and Henry Ford marketed the first affordable automobile. The 1930s brought the radio telescope and xerography, the 1940s the atomic bomb and supersonic aircraft, the 1950s the integrated circuit and the laser, and the 1960s the ARPANET—forerunner of the Internet—the minicomputer, and the handheld calculator. The personal computer was invented in the 1970s, the Internet and graphical user interface (GUI) made its appearance in the late 1980s, and the global positioning system (GPS) was deployed in the 1990s.

Each of these inventions rode on waves of innovation with specific beginnings, middles, and ends that generally overlapped one another—bringing the end products to us in close succession, like waves breaking on the shore.

Modern information technology rode its own wave of innovation that began in the 1940s with the introduction of the first general-purpose electronic computer—the ENIAC. By the 1960s, the IBM mainframe computer brought computing into the business world, where it blossomed. In the 1980s, the personal computer shrunk computers down to a size and price that made them manageable and affordable for use by individual employees, while progress in local area networks allowed them to be connected together. The 1990s brought the beginning of the widespread use of the Internet with the development of the World Wide Web. Today IT has become the basic backbone of the way commerce is done, changing the game forever and creating a huge WHY-do-anything dynamic.

## 40 Years of Technology Acceleration

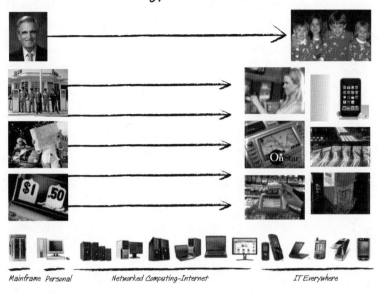

Mainframe Personal    Networked Computing-Internet    IT Everywhere

Figure 2

As you can see represented on the left side of Figure 2, the world in which I grew up was simple and slow moving. The world of my grandchildren—on the right side of Figure 2—is complex and always on. This transformation has taken just 40 years from beginning to end.

As these waves of innovation rolled in and left their mark, new enterprises emerged and old enterprises either changed or vanished. Enterprises will succeed on their ability to adapt and prosper, or they will fail as they calcify and wither. A key responsibility of any leadership team is to ensure that their enterprise survives and thrives. So what are the characteristics of a 21st century model?

Everyone is familiar with Aesop's fable about the tortoise and the hare. In this classic tale, a speedy hare is challenged to a race by a much slower tortoise. After leaping to an early lead, the hare—confident that there was no way the tortoise could catch up with and overtake him—decided to rest, and he soon fell asleep. While the hare was sleeping, the tortoise eventually caught up and passed him—ultimately winning the race. Aesop's fable ended with the familiar moral, "Slow and steady wins the race."

But is that particular assessment still true?

Many businesses today can be categorized as either hares or tortoises. The hares choose innovation and speed over all else, at the expense of leverage, quality, and consistency. The tortoises take a disciplined approach focusing on operational excellence and in doing so, they may miss out on new opportunities. Today's business environment, however, favors neither hares nor tortoises. The companies that will survive and thrive in the future are the ones that have the best attributes of both hares and tortoises—a hybrid of the two. Yet many enterprises cling to one model or the other. Or worse, they continue to bounce between the two with constant reorganizations.

These models and structures did not come out of thin air—they were originally based on necessity. In the early 1900s, as businesses expanded regionally, then nationally and internationally, it was extremely difficult to quickly communicate with outlying operations. There was no Internet, no email—initially, not even coast-to-coast telephone service. Manufacturing and distribution facilities just one state away from headquarters were basically on their own and by necessity ran independently. Internally, a division of labor—again, based on the Industrial model—meant that workers and departments were specialized and functional. Businesses changed and grew on the basis of analytical learning, studying the good examples and bad mistakes of others, and planning their strategies accordingly.

Some companies organized around geography (Frito-Lay, for example), others around product (like Procter & Gamble), and some around services (FedEx and others). All of these companies were—and still are—very successful. They are customer-centric and operationally excellent. However, all have had to reinvent themselves in recent years because consumers or retail customers (like Wal-Mart) do not care about Frito-Lay's geographies or Procter & Gamble's product companies. And guess what? They are not concerned with how your corporation is organized or how your P&L is structured, either. They just want to quickly and easily acquire your full product line with their supply-chain leverage, get it off the shelf and into consumers' shopping carts, and ring the register.

More important, the retailer can demand to do business with one Frito-Lay and one Procter & Gamble to achieve their supply-chain power and their own operational excellence. In the case of Wal-Mart, this means the right product at the right price, in the right store and location, at the right time. And by the right time, they mean right now. In other words, the supplier keeps the inventory carrying costs.

The real challenge today for a Frito-Lay or Procter & Gamble is that every one of their customers can demand to do business in a way that suits them. Ahold, Carrefour, Costco, Kroger, Target, Tesco, Wal-Mart, and other major retail chains have their own structures and processes that may or may not match the way product manufacturers need and expect to do business with them. That is where companies' agility must focus without destroying their own operational excellence.

To be successful in the 21st century, the supplier must quickly adjust to the customer, not the other way around. This holds true up and down the supply chain, with suppliers to Frito-Lay and Procter & Gamble adjusting and responding to them just as they must respond to their retailers. This creates the need for a very different and systematic approach to business, processes, systems, structures, metrics, cultures, and incentives.

In other words, a modern business model requires a modern systems model.

The global business environment is changing faster than ever before. Future success is clearly about speed, about setting a pace that gets you there before the competition—emulating the hare—and staying agile enough to adapt as the market fluctuates. But it is equally about being the tortoise—instilling discipline, operational excellence, standardization, simplification and automation, and focusing on serving the customer and making a profit in the process.

Most consumer-goods companies are quickly responding to this new dynamic and leading-edge corporations across other industries are not far behind.

However, many enterprises are still decentralized—either structurally due to a franchised or distributorship model, or out of tradition—and others are a rollup of many companies due to acquisitions. These old models are broken, and they will not continue to bring the organizations that cling to them the high levels of performance they will need to thrive in the 21st century. Many companies have begun their journey. But because IT is so central to the required business model changes, and because IT is still such a blind spot, these are high-risk investments today.

But do they still have to be in the future?

Successful modern enterprises have created a new competitive model that deals with the "and" versus the "either/or." These enterprises are simultaneously centralized for leverage, operational excellence, and global consistency—and decentralized for insightful decision-making, innovation, and speed.

To achieve sustainable competitiveness for the new era of global, always-on commerce, the enterprise and its systems, practices, incentives, and culture have to be structured around both speed and leverage—not one at the expense of the other. Today's most successful companies have adopted this new model. However, for those companies that have not yet taken the plunge, to achieve it will take time, investment, skill, and an iron will to change to the new dynamics of this century.

## Assets Are No Longer an Asset

The most successful companies of the last century owned and controlled most of their assets—their workforces, manufacturing plants, raw materials, and systems. Henry Ford was the founding father of revolutionary thinking in such industries. His fierce determination to be independent of suppliers drove him in the late 1920s to fabricate the largest, most efficient, integrated industrial complex in the world. Constructed along the Rouge River in Dearborn, Michigan, Ford's River Rouge complex sprawled across more than 2,000 acres with 90 miles of railroad track, 120 miles of conveyers, 53,000 machine tools, and 75,000 employees. It forged steel, stamped parts, and had its own power plant, glass works, cement kilns, and even a byproducts plant that produced charcoal.

Though it still operates—and is Ford's largest factory—River Rouge today is a shadow of its former self. It has been downsized to a 600-acre footprint with 6,000 workers, and many of its operations—such as steel production (currently owned by a Russian steelmaking concern)—have been sold off to other companies. In late 2006, Ford pledged its plants and assets—even its Blue Oval trademark—as collateral to secure a credit line of up to $25 billion to bankroll its turnaround.[2]

What happened? Owning "stuff" has become an impediment to speed and flexibility. Physical assets and complexity have become extremely costly in terms of time, agility, and resources. In the past, the more stuff a company owned, the more processes it controlled and the more powerful it was. Today, everything has flipped upside down. Owning buildings, workforce, physical inventories, and other such assets have become liabilities—rigid organization structures, vertical integration, and functionalism are the molasses of the 21st century enterprise.

Today, the less stuff an enterprise owns, the more powerful it is. This is because it possesses flexibility and agility—the muscles of the modern enterprise. Attuned organizations can quickly adapt via outsourcing—shifting work to suppliers, and spinning off clerical functions (self-service) to customers who often would rather do it themselves over the Internet. Power goes to those enterprises that can rapidly change the complexion of their businesses as the world ebbs and flows—reducing their costs and increasing their agility by incorporating consumer self-service technologies, global supply chain leverage, and a flexible workforce. These enterprises can push inventory and cost to their suppliers (an approach perfected by Wal-Mart) and have their customers do the work (as airlines have done) that buildings full

[2] Synovation Article – C Feld

of clerks and call center people used to do. If done right, the result can be higher levels of service and customer satisfaction and lower costs. They can also move work from one supplier to another—and from one continent to another—depending on availability, stability, economics, or quality.

Instead of a complex composite of assets and people, the successful 21st century enterprise is a virtual ecosystem that is always on and responsive to its customers in ways that old-line companies could never imagine.

Successful enterprises are constantly seeking new routes and models to stay a step ahead of the ever-changing marketplace and make the most of insights and knowledge from customers and business partners. Effective leaders are exploring how to work even more efficiently—smarter, faster, and better—and to allow quicker responses to competitive political and economic conditions. The lines are also blurring among how employees, suppliers, and customers interact. Customers are placing and tracking their own orders, suppliers are seamlessly connected to respond to those orders and requests, and many employees actually work for outsourcing partners in far-off lands.

In fact, an enterprise in a zero-latency world where answers and outputs are expected immediately cannot be described in 20th century terms at all. The old ways of talking about business—centralization vs. decentralization, SG&A vs. cost of revenue, and command/control vs. entrepreneurial—simply do not quite fit anymore. These changes are incomprehensible to many leaders, because the new enterprise is much faster moving and more transparent than they are used to. Inefficiencies are more evident to the customer, pricing is exposed, and switching to a competitor is significantly easier.

## The Modern Systems Approach: A "Core" Platform and a "Customer-Centric" Edge

In a market where most businesses are still organized in large, vertical departments, regions, or product divisions, today's most competitive enterprises are characterized by seamless outside-in horizontal processes and structures that are simple and globally consistent for their customers, partners, and workforces. The prevalent Industrial-era structure is one in which production schedules are driven by plans, not customers. Variations in demand are handled through costly excess inventories—or stockouts—and outputs are rigid, offering consumers little choice. They are characterized by a high-fixed, low-variable cost and are slow to respond to a fiercely competitive marketplace.

The organizations that are thriving today are those that have evolved away from their rigid, internally motivated structures and have adapted to the way customers want to interact with them. At the same time, they are focused on continuously simplifying, commonizing, and leveraging their operations core. They have also reversed their model to a less fixed, more variable cost structure, enabling them to be flexible and aggressive in their response to marketplace dynamics. To be competitive, organizations stuck with old, Industrial-era structures must undergo a fundamental transformation.

So how do these companies do it? What pioneering business model supports such an approach?

The ideal structure is a hybrid that supports both leverage and speed—one that pulls much of the operation into a systematic commonization and standardization of core processes. This creates a platform from which you can go to market locally or globally serving customers the way they want to be served.

This hybrid approach is counterintuitive to most companies because they have historically and purposefully designed for regional, product, or functional alignment. It is a model shift that requires a different mindset, a new way of approaching organizational excellence. In his books *Built to Last* and *Good to Great*, Jim Collins precisely expressed this shift when he reported that the corporate language of the 20th century was all about either/or—trying to choose between either centralization or decentralization, field or headquarters, innovation or leverage, and so on. The debate centers around the merits of each (centralization is bad, decentralization is good; overhead is bad, field is good; etc.). It's a discussion still going on in most 20th century enterprises, and the pendulum naturally swings back and forth over the years, based on the particular beliefs of the reigning executive team.

There's a fundamental problem with this debate: These are the wrong foundational words for the dialogue, the wrong focus for doing things right.

We live in a much more complex world, where "and" thinking must dominate our leadership patterns. The answer to the question "Do you want cost or quality?" is that you actually want both. The same is true with the questions "standardized or customized?," "regional or global?," "centralized or decentralized?," and so on. The answer is yes, yes, and yes. You want all those factors, but orchestrated in a way that is relevant to what and how people want to buy, how they want to be served, and how you can make money.

The true discussion should be centered on one basic foundation: "How do I gain market share and competitively grow? And how do I make money doing it?" In other words, "What gives me cost and quality leverage and what gives me speed and flexibility in the marketplace? How do I grow revenue and margin in a competitive global economy?"

## Everything's Going the Wrong Way

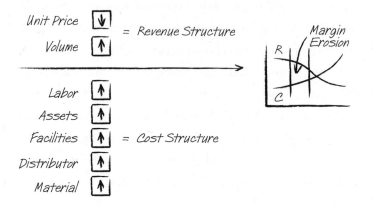

The Home Depot is a good example of a decentralized model that was extremely successful during the latter part of the 20th century but needed a new model as the competition and the customers both changed.

## 3C CASE STUDY
# The Home Depot

Wal-Mart has been one of America's great business success stories, and for good reason. When Wal-Mart, headquartered in Bentonville, Arkansas, began to grow in 1970, the company was, by design, Bentonville-centric—all of the power, information systems, and common processes emanated out of Bentonville. This was the Sam Walton model of doing business. Sam's model was very centralized, and initially individual store managers did not have much in the way of decision rights. Stores were extensions of the parent organization—they stocked whatever the company sent them, and they stocked it in a very specific way. The business model was highly leveraged, with a common way of doing procurement through store management.

If you were a Wal-Mart vendor—as I was as CIO of Frito-Lay—you quickly understood the power of their model. They would bring you to Bentonville and forcefully explain the Wal-Mart way. Even a big brand like Fritos—with a large national market share—had to concede if it wanted to play in Wal-Mart's stores. If you did not want to do business their way, then your growth would be very limited with the nation's fastest-growing retail outlet. While they might have to give you some shelf space—because their customers were looking for Frito products—they would not give you very much, or would not place you in a prominent location, and they would go to a private label or to your regional competitors to fill out their shelves. It was and remains today a phenomenal model of purchasing power.

### Sam's Model

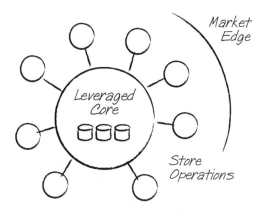

At Home Depot, however, Arthur Blank and Bernie Marcus had the opposite idea. Their philosophy and business model was that the store was supreme—that the store manager knew more about what items to carry in the store. In the case of Home Depot, the Atlanta headquarters took a back seat to the individual stores. Other than the brand itself—the orange box, the look and feel—

little in the store was driven out of Atlanta. The person who ran the store knew the customers, and he or she knew what they wanted far better than anyone at headquarters.

## Arthur & Bernie's Model

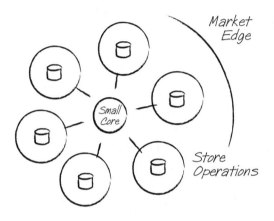

Home Depots were designed to compete with the local hardware stores and the power and processes to do so effectively were put into every store. If a store manager wanted to stock a particular American Standard fixture because that's what his customers wanted, he could do it—no questions asked. Suppliers called on store managers and decisions were made locally. The downside of the model was that the American Standard fixture stocked by one store was likely to have a different part number than the same American Standard fixture stocked by another store. There were no centralized databases and little in the way of centralized procurement, and therefore limited leverage with suppliers. Home Depot had great customer touch, but no purchasing leverage in their $50+ billion franchise.

The company grew one store at a time. Following Arthur and Bernie's model, Home Depot became one of the great retail growth stories of the '80s and '90s. However, like Frito-Lay, the company began to see "clouds on the horizon" as a powerful new competitor—Lowe's—began its explosive growth. After a while, you could hardly find a Home Depot that did not have a Lowe's nearby, under construction, or planned.

Although Home Depot was still very successful—with a plan to double the number of stores and enter new marketplaces— Lowe's was taking away market share at an alarming rate and Wal-Mart continued to add hardware items to its franchise. As a result, the Home Depot board hired Bob Nardelli to reenergize the company's competitiveness. Nardelli was from GE, where the Jack Welch's data-driven, Six Sigma, boundaryless, global-thinking model was in full swing.

Nardelli quickly understood the supply-chain leverage that was lost by Home Depot's decentralized, store-centric model. He and his new team believed that for the company to continue to profitably expand the franchise, increase their competitiveness, gain back market share and restart growth, they needed to shift their supply-chain power from the store managers to the Atlanta Headquarters. He also saw the need for new Internet-enabled marketing channels in addition to the company's traditional orange-box stores. More important, Nardelli wanted customers and transactions to flow seamlessly between channels and stores, so customers could buy an item on the Web and pick it up at whatever store had the item in stock—or buy an item in one store and return it to another.

Nardelli and his team immediately grasped the WHY-change dynamics. They brought The Feld Group in to consult on the WHAT and HOW with them and Bob DeRodes, Home Depot's new CIO. We assigned two of our best and brightest: Stan

Alexander and Keith Halbert. We agreed that Home Depot's original business model, although successful, was becoming less competitive as Lowe's and others began to expand. However, Home Depot's current-state model also had some very good store-level customer internal capabilities that needed to be preserved. We realized that a more-modern hybrid model of a centralized core platform for supply chain leverage tethered to a market-centric store manager influence was the ideal model. In fact, that is exactly how Wal-Mart evolved over the '90s.

To succeed, we needed to build a cohesive plan for the new collaborative Home Depot and help them take the company on a systemic, multiyear journey—aligning the store managers' incentives, systems, and company culture around this new model.

### Home Depot Journey

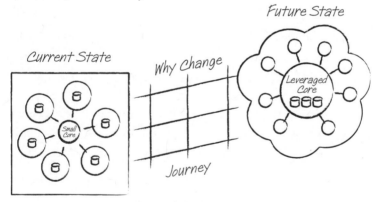

Although Home Depot had a solid WHY-change agenda, the leadership team began to rapidly change the business model without pacing the systems, processes, culture, and incentives. You cannot start to make decisions in Atlanta without having the processes in place to support a centralized supply chain and being able to see the information showing what was going on in the stores. The problem was that Home Depot's information systems were decentralized, their IT infrastructure and data so fragmented, and their processes so individually store centric, that the magnitude of the effort in every dimension was daunting. They were a $50+ billion business with the muscle tone of 1,500 separate $35 million businesses.

Nevertheless, Nardelli's team was convinced they needed to move ahead at full throttle. As a result, during that timeframe you could go into a Home Depot store and some shelves would be empty, while other shelves had more stuff than they'd ever sell in a year's time. Loyal store managers and customers became frustrated. They had a very strong WHY change and a good conceptual WHAT to change to but struggled because they immediately rotated the axis of decision rights (WHO) before they implemented the process changes, information flows, and access. Had there been, in addition to their compelling WHY change, a more well-defined WHAT to change to—along with a reasonably paced path to execution—I believe the Home Depot transformation would have been faster and more successful.

I have seen during my career both bad ideas poorly executed and good ideas well executed. Unfortunately, this was a good idea poorly executed, and it ultimately forced the Home Depot board to change management and rethink its approach. Some would argue that the company had to move as quickly as it did because they began very late. I would argue that properly pacing the execution is as critical as having the right idea.

Here is the so what of the Home Depot and Wal-Mart models that companies struggle with. It is not about centralization versus decentralization—both have their virtues and liabilities. It is about common versus unique processes, standard versus disjointed information, and leveraged versus fragmented IT platforms and networks. If you are common, standard, and leveraged in your systems, data, and processes, you can continuously flex between centralized and decentralized where it is appropriate, like Wal-Mart. However, if those things are unique, disjointed, and fragmented, you are locked into those structures and change is expensive and slow, like Home Depot's was.

It is a simple change in a Wal-Mart or Frito-Lay type model to further evolve the organization. For example, over the years both have given more decision rights to the store managers and route salesmen because now they've got a lot of stores in a lot of different kinds of neighborhoods with different tastes and preferences. Moving from a highly centralized to a modern hybrid model has worked well for both companies. The principle is that if your systems are standardized and processes commonized, then your decision-making can easily flow between centralization or decentralization—or some hybrid in between. It is actually what agility or flexibility in an uncertain world is about.

It may seem counterintuitive, but the more standardized your systems and processes are, the more flexible you can be. Wal-Mart was able to quickly react to changing market conditions because of its systemic commonization. It had the systems and the databases in place needed to support the change. Home Depot was unable to quickly react to its changing market conditions because of its decentralized systems and processes. Their entire platform needed to be transformed before the company could be changed.

I tell the Home Depot story because they got the WHY change, but moved too fast. Recognizing WHY you need to change—and making it compelling and urgent to your leadership team, employees, and investors—is the first and most important foundational step in the journey. But, if you get that right, then you must quickly articulate an inspiring destination for your enterprise—the WHAT, and a path to execution: the HOW.

# CHAPTER 4

WHY     WHAT     HOW     WHO

**THE WHAT**

# WHAT Will We Do?

The WHAT to change (WHAT will we do?). Assuming the WHY change is compelling and can be articulated, it becomes critical to describe what actually needs to change. It is equally important to describe what needs to stay the same. These conversations naturally gravitate toward centralization versus decentralization themes. A more appropriate dialogue should be focused on what gives you speed and customer centricity, and what gives you scale, leverage, and quality. This plank should fundamentally describe your future-state business model and be extremely agile.

## 4A THE FRITO-LAY JOURNEY
# WHAT We Did

As we focused Frito-Lay on regional combat, we deleveraged the valuable national platform of purchasing, manufacturing, and distribution. Bill Korn proved that, regionally, we could grow market share and revenue, but our cost structure and legendary flawless execution flipped upside down. As a result, we missed our plan. Since there were no points for second place at PepsiCo, Bill was replaced by Mike Jordan, who had been moved to the position of president of PepsiCo, and was asked to return as CEO of Frito-Lay.

Under Mike, our leadership team concluded that Bill was half right. Regional focus was the way to attack the market if we were to grow market share and revenue. But it was more subtle than just pure regionalism, because many of the larger chains such as

Wal-Mart, Kroger, and Safeway had become national for their own scale leverage. Some wanted to be served nationally, some regionally, and the really sophisticated ones wanted national purchasing power, but regional execution.

Wal-Mart wanted everyday low prices and did not care about our pricing and promotion calendar. Kroger wanted our promotions to coincide with their regional market areas, while Safeway, 7-11, and Ralph's wanted different schemes altogether. Because they had all begun to leverage their purchasing power, that put pressure on our pricing. But it also put pressure on our cost structure because of the complexity of "having it their way." That complexity rippled through our computer systems, route trucks, and plants. It really went beyond regional to customer-by-customer—or what we called "segment-of-one."

We also needed to focus on our own cost and quality, which had its roots in our national scale, leverage, and operational excellence—that is, if we wanted to make money while serving our customers in new ways. The WHAT requirements were then established. Could we enable segment-of-one customization and maintain our national, leveraged model?

## Frito-Lay Journey

Over the next few months we designed a hybrid WHAT framework that was very commonized and standardized in systems, processes, and tools; it was national in our core operations, and empowered at the market-edge to serve customer and regional differences. That is easy to say and it sounds great in a speech, but it was too high level for an actual business-model-change program. Back then, you were either centralized with the proper planning and control systems and accountabilities in place to support command and control from the mother ship, or you were decentralized—letting a thousand ideas blossom because the people at the edge were accountable only to their region's or product's profitability. The technology of that era was limited and molded around the organizational format: either centralized mainframes or distributed mini-computers.

Our design was a hybrid based on what truly gave us operational excellence, economies of scale, and customer-level flexibility. It raised questions like: How do we structure processes, information systems, decision rights, and incentives so that flexibility at the market edge does not destroy our economics or core execution? That model was used to generate business requirements and it outlined the things that we needed to change and—as important—things that would remain the same.

A key component was Area Business Teams (ABT), consisting of a highly matrixed senior team in each geographic region. This team was a microcosm of the executive committee with each major function having a seat at the table. They had split objectives between their headquarters' functional leaders (i.e. manufacturing, purchasing, etc.) and their Area Business Team leaders (West, East, South, etc.). The design of required information systems kept pointing toward a more-flexible system—a centralized national core (procurement, manufacturing, and distribution) and a decentralized customer edge (sales and marketing). Fortunately for us, like Wal-Mart, we were already centralized and functionalized so we had a great jumpstart for the national core. So our main focus would be on enabling sales and marketing at the edge. We now had our WHAT, and it was time to go execute it.[3]

[3] Harvard Business School Case Study Frito-Lay Inc.: A Strategic Transition (Consolidated) July, 1993

## 4B
# WHAT Will We Do?

If you take some time to reflect on the Frito-Lay example, you will probably realize there is some heavy lifting required for the executive leadership team to begin to shape the direction that you want to take your enterprise. This is more than the compulsory financial exercise that investors demand, or the cursory budget ritual of setting targets and allocating resources. It is a deep, far-ranging, top-to-bottom assessment that has the potential to dramatically change the way your organization does business—and its future prospects for continuing to do so well.

At a minimum, you have to articulate how you are going to achieve the numbers—more stores, more routes, new acquisitions, new products, new channels, and increased productivity targets. However, in well-run companies, this goes beyond the numbers and into the soul of the value proposition: What are your beliefs about the future? What do you want to be known for? How will you serve your customers? Who are your competitors? How will you partner with your suppliers? What are your aspirations for the employee experience? How will government policy affect your operation, economics, and more?

In short, what are your business's beliefs? And what would your future business model look like in a modern world? How will you continue to not just survive, but also thrive in this continuously changing landscape?

## Defining the Future State

Customers want a lot from companies, but remember: What a customer wants must include what they ultimately are willing to pay for. That specific requirement must become the focus of all dialogues within the organization—the logic of which lends itself to a set of durable principles that can help define the future state. These principles can best be described by asking four questions:

### 1. Who are your customers?

Who are your direct customers, and how are they buying from you? Do they want to buy locally, regionally, and/or globally? Through what channels? Delivered how? And delivered when?

### 2. Who are you?

Are you in one business or many businesses? What components of your business can be leveraged, and what is truly different from your competition? These facets should begin to define your core operation and your customer-centric-edge.

For example, Westinghouse was in multiple industries—nuclear power (Westinghouse Electric Company), furniture (Knoll Group), entertainment (CBS), and others, with very little leverage. Home Depot is in the retail hardware business—but what looks like one business has multiple channels, including those big orange-box stores (consumer retail), builder direct (wholesale), consumer online, and contractor services (connecting customers with Home Depot partners in areas such as fencing, construction, and installation) with significant core leverage.

**3. Who are your competitors?**

Who are your primary competitors, and are they gaining or losing market share and margin? How are your competitors organized and run? Who are your emerging competitors, and what non-traditional approaches are they taking? Where are they coming from—locally, regionally, and globally?

**4. Who are your key suppliers?**

Are your key suppliers local, regional, or global—or some combination thereof? What is your required cycle time? Is the raw material perishable or durable? Is it readily available or scarce? Is it a quick or slow cycle to your demand side?

As you look at these organizing principles and begin to describe your business from the outside in, the foundation of your modern business model should begin to emerge. Operations and processes that drive leverage and operational excellence to those efforts should define your core platform. That core needs to be standardized, simplified, and automated to the point that the operations and processes can be globally consistent, including functions that are not fully owned by you such as joint ventures. This ecosystem should be run as a virtual core, even though it may be physically or financially separate from your center.

At Frito-Lay, the core for us was our supply chain, manufacturing, and distribution systems. They truly gave us leverage and were engineered for operational excellence.

Tethered to this core foundation of consistent processes and systems are the more flexible structures that give your company speed and visibility in the changing market. This is your customer-centric edge. Unlike the central core, your operational models can be in constant flux, adapting to the way the markets and your customers want to interact. These might take the form of anything from account teams to regional-product or service-line P&Ls delivered through websites, kiosks, smartphones, and other platforms. However you structure your market edge, decision makers working within it must have the ability to influence pricing, promotions, and other localized programs.

At Frito-Lay, this flexible edge had to empower our sales and marketing functions since regional variations mattered and product pricing and promotions needed to be at the customer level. That business architecture positioned us to react immediately from the point-of-transaction edge and plug into our leveraged core for both economies of scale and consistent quality. This blueprint re-created the entrepreneurial business model, but on a scalable, leveraged platform.

This modern business architecture has many advantages, allowing your enterprise to:

- Quickly launch innovative marketplace programs from the edge

- Create continuous improvement from the center core
- Flex up and down, because you've adjusted the fixed/variable structure
- Leverage your global supply chain to take advantage of scale
- Operate in a targeted, customized way at the point of sale

The core platform strengthens the organization through consistency—marketing can present a unified brand and identity, supply chain can take advantage of economies of scale, and delivery can quickly deploy predetermined solutions to any customer problem. The entire enterprise is elevated as a result.

Further, this approach allows decentralized decisions to move to the field where they can be implemented most effectively. Using a military example, the core elements and battle plans are provided by central command, ensuring that the entire battalion moves in concert. Field officers are then well equipped and sure of their direction and support structures. This frees them to focus on localized strategy and changing conditions that may not be visible at the center.

This hybrid model—combining a strong central core with a flexible market edge—is becoming an increasingly crucial element in customer service and customer relationship management. Because customers can now access and respond to information almost instantaneously—primarily through the Internet—they have learned to expect immediate interactions. They also want those experiences to be personalized and customized which is a tough challenge for companies dealing with literally millions of people every day.

Even more difficult is that some customers want a global approach, while some still like and expect a local or regional flavor. Many are motivated by a deal that only a leveraged supply chain can deliver, while others are looking for good value and partnership at a reasonable price. A company that operates with a strong core platform and a market-centric edge has flexibility to meet all of those diverse demands creating a feeling of customization consisting of standard building blocks.

Remember that you are not just selling a product or service—you are building a relationship. It takes very little to move a customer from being your biggest advocate and brand champion to switching to a competitor. And, in today's Web 2.0 environment, an individual can spread his or her thoughts—both good or bad—almost immediately across social networks and online communities, reaching hundreds or even thousands of readers within minutes of posting.

Adopting this modern business architecture helps you optimize customer relationships. For each step in the value chain—from the first moment customers learn about your company, to the time a satisfied customer becomes a repeat buyer—you have an opportunity to enhance their satisfaction and loyalty. By capturing localized information throughout key processes— sales, marketing, delivery, customer service, and other functional areas—and analyzing that information across the enterprise, your entire company can quickly respond to the market and stay ahead of the curve.

For example, in the old 20th century model, retail chains typically allowed stores to operate autonomously—as was the case with the pre-Nardelli Home Depot described in the previous chapter. Corporate offices provided air coverage such as national advertising, distribution routes, and basic support functions. But most processes and operations were handled within each local store. It seemed like a good concept, as each manager could adjust inventory to meet the neighborhood's demands. Stores also had sales and specials that were specifically tailored to appeal to their unique customer base.

But while the relationships benefited the business and the customer who generally went to one neighborhood store, they did not leverage scale and purchasing power, missing out on a key competitive advantage. And, as Internet and shopping malls were added into the mix, these rigid one-to-one relationships actually became a liability.

In today's model, local stores share the intelligence they collect with the central core operation. Data is captured on demographics, buying preferences, new interests, and customer requests. Similar data comes from other localities. As trends emerge across the board, the central core can quickly adjust its supply chain power and distribution, launch new products and promotions that get to market faster, and rapidly disseminate better planning criteria back to the front line. The customer relationship is with the company through any channel—not with just one store.

This new hybrid model—disciplined enough to stick to a path but flexible enough to adjust to the landscape—will win most every time.[4] To sort through how your enterprise should structure its processes for the future, you should use an unconstrained wide-aperture lens. Looking in your rearview mirror to decide what to do in the future is dangerous. At the same time, focusing on the hood ornament of a car at high speed can land you in a ditch. It is too close in and short term for this effort.

[4] Synovations – C Feld

Instead, this effort requires looking at where the markets, technology, legislation, competitors, politics, consumers, employers, suppliers, and economics are going. What are the patterns and where are the rapids running? These questions will help you outline your beliefs about the future. From there you can determine the vision and strategy that will then become the framework for the WHAT that will drive your business model.

This is not an IT exercise. It is predominately a business-driven program that uses technology to leverage its power. You do not have to know .NET or JAVA or the difference between SAP and Oracle. It is all about a clear, understandable articulation of the business content and context, processes, rules, decision rights, and incentives.

In short, it is about what I have referred to as your business architecture.

## 4C CASE STUDY
# Burlington Northern Santa Fe

Let me illustrate this notion with the story of the way we built our business architecture at the Burlington Northern Santa Fe Railroad around beliefs about the future, how it was articulated to the board of directors, and how the company has moved into the 21st century as a result.

My first engagement after starting The Feld Group upon leaving Frito-Lay was with the Burlington Northern Railroad in 1992. The company's chairman and CEO Jerry Grinstein had given me a call to talk about his frustration with his IT organization. Being in Fort Worth, Texas, he was familiar with the technology systems we had implemented at Frito-Lay and had gotten my name from a mutual friend. Jerry was an affable executive who had taken over a failing railroad in the late '80s, taken it out of debt, and was now trying to figure out a way to grow it profitably.

He began describing the colorful history of a company within an industry that helped build the economic fabric of the United States as commerce pushed westward during the 19th and 20th centuries. The railroad industry is unique and capital-intensive. Unlike the trucking industry where the government built the interstate highway system, the rail industry had to build and maintain its own track—which is in constant need of re-investment. Grinstein showed me a sample of track that was brand new and one that had been in use for some time. The actual wearing down of the metal after it had been in use for a couple of years was striking. It was a palpable example of what depreciation looks like. The net effect of track depreciation was that trains could run significantly faster on a new track than after it was worn.

However, compared to a consumer-goods company within an extremely competitive marketplace that had significant systems intensity, the railroad looked like you could plan it on the back of a napkin and execute it without a single computer. And as for the competitive environment it was a virtual monopoly since only the Burlington Northern (BN) could move on BN track through BN territory. It was so backward relative to Frito-Lay that in 1992 the crews that drove through certain areas of the country were still receiving Indian pay—even though there had not been a train attacked by Indians in more than 100 years.

However, Jerry had such a strong vision of a 21st century company and a rebirth of the rail industry that it was infectious. The industry had been deregulated in the 1970s and—because rail service was so unreliable, and the costs of some of these archaic practices continued to weigh on the railroads—trucking (on government-funded highways) had taken a huge dent out of the rail business. Jerry's vision was easy to articulate: He was going to run a scheduled railroad with committed service-delivery windows to take back market share lost to trucking—and do it in a cost-competitive way.

The minute I heard Jerry's vision for Burlington Northern, the importance of systems and technology jumped out and grabbed me. Although easy to articulate and grasp, this journey was going to be extremely difficult to execute. I agreed to help Burlington Northern lay out an IT plan and to articulate the business architecture into a strategy to modernize the company. A scheduled, disciplined, on-time railroad required that you know exactly where every locomotive is physically, which cars are connected to that locomotive, and what is in each car—and where each car is going and to whom. In other words, a real-time picture of the physical movements of the entire system.

Our first step was to take about 30 days to do a CAT scan of the then-current state of BN's systems and processes. It was clear that IT systems did not reflect in a reliable, real-time way where the assets were or where they were going.

### Different at any one time
Current State

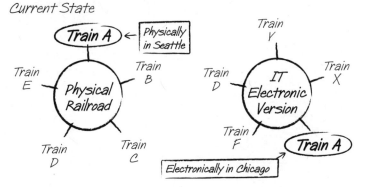

Our next step was to take 30 days to understand the future state of what it would take to achieve the "scheduled railroad."

## Realtime - In perfect synchronization

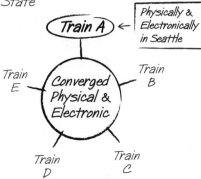

Finally, once we got agreement on both the current and future states, we took the next 30 days and articulated the path—and the organizational pain—required to get from one to the other.

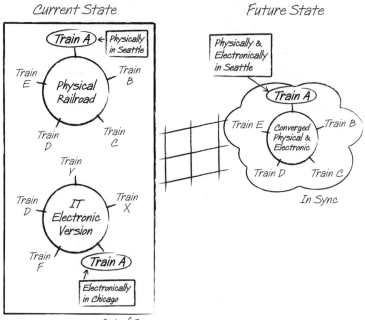

This included rough estimates of timing and costs, along with an assessment of potential risks and changes required to the business and organization. Since this initiative was going to be both risky and expensive, we had to go to BN's board of directors to gain their support and approval.

So in just the fourth month of working with Grinstein and his team—prepared and bubbling with enthusiasm—I found myself and my systems team waiting to enter the BN board meeting at the City Club in Fort Worth. It was a very distinguished board that included, among others, Congresswoman Barbara Jordan. And, as you may remember from her work on the House Judiciary Committee, her questions were always very penetrating.

Despite the board's qualifications, most of the members were not railroad people—they were business people, lawyers, and politicians. We were given just two hours to try to convince them that BN should embark on this IT systems journey at great risk, effort, and expense—that indeed it was essential to Burlington Northern's survival that they do so. I was a little concerned about how to capture these non-IT leaders in a narrow two-hour window before the board dinner, but I was eager to present what we had learned in the previous 90 days. We believed that once the board understood how primitive their IT systems were, Burlington Northern would be ready to get to work.

I began by telling the board a story about Coors, one of BN's biggest customers. Coors is based in Golden, Colorado, because of the spring water that gives their beer its distinctive taste. This approach meant that Coors had to have a central manufacturing complex in Golden in tandem with a very extensive distribution system. Coors was a captive client of BN because it was the railroad that ran by their complex. We were a main artery for Coors because the company needed to ship lots of stuff—in a constant stream—in and out of their beer-making facilities.

On the inbound side were the grains, hops, coal, metal, glass, and packaging required to produce beer—by the trainload. On the outbound side was climate-controlled beer. Trains moved in and out of Coors' manufacturing facilities continuously—24 hours a day, 7 days a week, 365 days a year. We were so integrated with one another that BN's trains served as a veritable Coors warehouse on wheels.

Sounds like a business marriage made in heaven, right?

Wrong.

Unfortunately, for Coors, BN treated each of the commodities required for the manufacture of its beer like it was a separate company. So Coors had to call a particular department in BN— with its own staff, way of doing business, and phone number—to schedule delivery of grain. To schedule a coal delivery required calling a different BN department at a different phone number, and there was yet another department and number to call to track the actual progress of deliveries. Coors had to deal with seven or eight different departments within Burlington Northern to get what it wanted, and several different operations groups to actually get things picked up, tracked, and delivered. And I do mean different—each department had separate telephone numbers, pricing departments, processes, databases, and—in many cases—corporate cultures. The grain people did not mix much with the coal desk, which did not have much reason to interact with the folks who tracked shipments.

We walked the board through a typical Coors transaction, showing the inefficiencies and customer frustrations that resulted from dealing with so many different organizations within Burlington Northern. We then moved the board to the next process. Once Coors got a price, they (the customer) had to call yet a different phone number to schedule a delivery. I can still remember Ms. Jordan exclaim in her booming voice, "You've got to be making this up!" I also remember Jerry responding in his jovial way, "That was the easy part. Wait until you see how we manage the execution of the delivery."

We were already halfway into our allotted two hours, but because of the questions, only one-quarter of the way through our storyline.

We next described to the board how the BN scheduling people would have to call train yards around the country to track down individual rail cars to see if they were empty or not. Once they found the cars they were looking for, they would then call Dispatch to have them sent to the right place to pick up the grain and deliver it to Coors. But the dispatchers did not know precisely where the cars were—they only knew if a car was in their yard, or if it had just left. After that, it was anyone's guess until the cars showed up in another yard.

As it turned out, BN had two kinds of rail yards—high tech and low tech. We described to the board how—in the low-tech version—one person would stand outside with a pair of binoculars and call out the numbers painted onto the sides of the railcars to another person standing next to him. That person would then write the numbers down, and whenever he got a chance, the information would be keyed into a terminal and transmitted to the main BN computer. As we showed the board, it could be hours—and sometimes an entire shift—before the data was entered. By that time the car was no longer there and the data was already obsolete.

The problem in a nutshell became immediately apparent to everyone in the room—the electronic representation of where things were in Burlington Northern's thousands of miles of track had nothing to do with the actual physical version. And that's why BN could not guarantee that a delivery would happen on any particular day. They sometimes could not even guarantee arrival within a week. That was because they had very little idea of where their 100,000+ railcars over 30,000 miles of track actually were at any given time.

Whenever one part of the system slowed down, Coors ran the risk of having to shut down their manufacturing plant. People dream of this type of supply-chain integration, but almost daily the dream turned into a nightmare for both companies.

This information got the board's attention. To say they found it hard to believe that in 1992 we were using binoculars to track railroad cars would be a major understatement. We were now entering Hour Three of our presentation, and the staff was getting nervous because the board was scheduled to start their dinner. However, dinner was the last thing on their minds. The board members were so engaged with our presentation—asking questions and getting involved along the way—that we had not even had the chance to tell them how we intended to go about fixing the railroad's problems, how long it would take, and how much it would cost. I remember Grinstein asking them if they wanted to stop for dinner and in unison they exclaimed, "No!"

The reality was we had been talking with the board about information technology issues for more than two hours and we had not once mentioned any IT jargon. It was all about business and process in a way that everyone could understand and engage in.

So, in Hour Three of our presentation, I began to move into the "And here is how we would fix it" part of the meeting. One of the board members interrupted me and said, "You just covered the low-tech yards. Tell me about the high-tech ones."

I am not sure what they were expecting to hear about the high-tech yards—perhaps that we had computerized scanning and tracking in place that sent railcar tracking data to Burlington Northern's headquarters in near-real time. Unfortunately, this was far from the case. I described to the board the typical setup at a high-tech yard, which comprised of videotape cameras that recorded the trains as they went by. As videotapes were recorded, the yardmaster—the employee in charge of the entire yard's operations—was responsible for watching the resulting video on a monitor and entering the data into the yard's computer system. The yardmaster could slow the tape down and key in the data whenever he got to it. The operative part of the last sentence is "whenever he got to it," because the yardmaster had plenty of other (what he probably considered more important) responsibilities besides watching the videotapes and keying in the railcar-tracking data.

So the problem of tracking was not really any better in a high-tech yard than it was in a low-tech one—it was just done without binoculars and with one less person. Sometimes it took even longer for the data to get into the system in a high-tech yard than it did in a low-tech yard where there were two people with binoculars in charge of gathering the information.

I had their attention. We had taken two-and-a-half hours to graphically explain what we had learned by observing their current-state CAT scan. Ms. Jordan sat there shaking her head in disbelief. She said in a serious tone, "Surely you have a solution." Grinstein chimed in, "If we want to compete with trucking and grow our business, we have to change the service delivery system from 'We'll get it there when it gets there,' to a more disciplined, scheduled railroad. To do that we have to change everything in our organizational structure and mindset, our processes and incentives, and our technology."

The competition was killing them. If we did not make the investment in the necessary system changes we would be relegated to be a coal-and-grain operation—the only commodities that cannot be economically moved on trucks. Following Grinstein's lead, I described what a modern, competitive railroad would look like—a railroad where the physical was precisely reflected in the electronic system.

Each of BN's railcars would be continuously tracked throughout the system by applying toll tag transponder technology to each car and placing readers across the railroad. Since we would know where everything was in near-real time, we could centralize dispatch in Fort Worth and everyone could have an accurate view of the entire railroad all of the time.

## Running a Scheduled Railroad

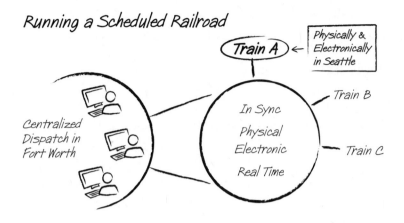

We broke the railroad down into its core and market-edge business processes, and showed the board an interaction model between Customers, Train Operations, Pricing and Scheduling, and Back Office. Instead of having 27 different departments within Burlington Northern—each with their own systems— we called for the implementation of just four major integrated systems data and processes, all focused on customer service. We showed that everything required could be contained in a system that had good data, a simple architecture, and applications that took the data and made it useable by operators, dispatchers, safety people, and others within the company who needed it.

We then walked the board through the same Coors transaction we had used to open the meeting, but this time using the new system. In our approach, Coors would have a single point of contact and a seamless service experience. They could order their own moves, track them from end to end, and both Coors and BN could reduce their costs and improve their quality. We had worked up a few metrics around justification, such as asset utilization through improved cycle times, reductions through staff consolidation, and truck-like pricing for truck-like service windows. We also laid out a schedule for a two-to-four-year effort along with an estimate of the investment required.

The board told us to go ahead. "We have no choice if we want to profitably grow."

That was the easy part. The hard part was taking the simplicity of the idea—the business and IT system design—and making it happen.

To turn his vision into reality, Jerry hired Ron Rittenmeyer who had partnered with me as the business operator that transformed Frito-Lay by leveraging the handheld technology. Ron was a unique executive who possessed a range of capabilities not often found in the same person. He had both the strategic ability to see the patterns and set a vision, and the operational, hands-on street smarts to understand how to execute the plan. In addition, he had the toughness needed to relentlessly drive major change programs and the fairness and integrity to do it the right way. Since Ron and I had worked together before, there was trust and confidence that building out the details required to execute the plan—versus the 90-day sketch needed to sell the idea—could be achieved. In addition to working on a detailed design with us, he also had to begin to change the organization, culture, incentives, union rules, and—in a number of cases—leadership.

Many IT investments fail or fall short because they are positioned as IT projects, when in reality they are business-change initiatives that require IT enablement. This is particularly true when you are defining the WHY change and WHAT your business architecture should be.

As we began our initiatives at Burlington Northern, we had a couple of good breaks. Toll tags were in the process of being mandated by the Interstate Commerce Commission, so we designed automatic readers and systems that would let you know where the trains were every time they passed the readers. And in September 1995—in the middle of our transformation—BN merged with the Santa Fe Railroad (SF) to form BNSF: Burlington Northern Santa Fe. As it turned out, Rob Krebs—chairman and CEO of the Santa Fe Railroad—had already made a big investment in IT built around a similar vision of our scheduled railroad, and we were able to use large portions of it. That gave us the acceleration to accomplish the most modern scheduled railroad—fully merged—within two years.

Today, if you stand in the control room of Burlington Northern Santa Fe's central headquarters in Fort Worth, Texas, you'll think you're looking at something run by NASA. The control room is almost the size of a football field. Fourteen giant video screens are arrayed across one wall, flashing constant updates of real-time data about the railroad in every conceivable configuration. Visitors can watch the control room from an observation deck and grasp the teamwork and precision execution of an extremely complex nervous system in operation.

But the real action is down on the floor, which is built to withstand a Category 5 hurricane, a major earthquake, or a severe tornado. What you see there are hundreds of monitors—each tracking trains in real-time, showing where they are on the track, where they are headed, when they will arrive, and what is in them. The toll tag edge-technology readers have been enhanced by a new edge technology: Global Positioning System (GPS), which gives the system a real-time, videogame feel.

BNSF has also added a number of Internet-enabled, self-service applications and is working on managing train control and positive train separation using the GPS technology. There is RFID (edge) technology within the West Coast ports, enabling BNSF to be an efficient gateway to China and a major player in global commerce.

Today, BNSF can tell its clients exactly where their railcars are, when they will arrive, and how much they will cost. Their customers can track the cars themselves, following the progress of their deliveries on the Internet. The physical railroad and the virtual railroad are now completely in sync. BNSF's transformation was not achieved in an annual budget cycle or with a risky big-bang major investment. It was a slow-and-steady, multiyear process—and it has turned out to be extremely durable.

You can see that BNSF's problem was predominately one of business and process integration. Starting and focusing on the HOW of technology without also considering WHAT you want to do is a high-risk, low-reward approach for your operation. The CIO can and must play an active role in helping articulate the vision—and in many cases lead the systems thinking and design. But this is predominately a business leadership function.

The vision should be the starting point of the effort to build a business architecture because it is the context for the rest of the effort. But you also need strong business partners to provide momentum. Many executive teams today are struggling because things are moving so rapidly—committing to any strategy or structure can reduce flexibility. This is where the discussion of the core platform versus the market-centric edge comes in. The core platform should be very durable—like at BNSF—while the market programs and pricing should be extremely flexible.

The durable-core category includes tangible things such as capital assets, locations, brands, and so forth. They usually transcend decades, leadership changes, organizational ebbs and flows, and the other variables that perish or are continuously reshaped. For example, Frito-Lay has reorganized a dozen times in the last 20 years, but the network of plants, distribution centers, suppliers, route trucks and their customers' store locations—although they have grown—are very durable, dependable and slow to change.

What does change more rapidly are pricing, promotions, marketing programs, bag sizes, products, flavors, and the like. Understanding, articulating, and designing for these different functions and dynamics is the basis of the business architecture— the WHAT. In the end, from Herman's day until now, Frito-Lay is essentially a make, move, and sell business. Separating organization from process is the key to a lasting architecture.

Efforts to improve the core platform should be focused on continuous simplification, process thinning, and automation. This will drive the cost-and-quality equation for the entire enterprise, and will be as agile and flexible as possible relative to lowering fixed costs and leveraging suppliers and workforce.

The best way to achieve operational excellence is to boil down the business to its simplest form—to distill its most vital essence. This in essence is what the founder does at the start up of a new company.

At BNSF, it is vital to know where everything is all of the time as did James Hill—founder of the Great Northern Railway, which ultimately became BNSF after a series of mergers. At Frito-Lay it is the Herman Lay model. A more recent example is Southwest Airlines. The Southwest Airlines model has its roots in company co-founder Herb Kelleher who started out more than 35 years ago with three planes flying six daily roundtrips between Dallas and San Antonio, and twelve daily roundtrips between Dallas and Houston. Kelleher knew his customers and his employees, and he had an intimate partnership with his suppliers.

Since Herb could see and be personally involved in every aspect and event of this small operation, he was able to serve his customers at every touch point. Selling customers a ticket, checking their bags, boarding them onto a plane, managing the in-flight experience, deplaning them at their destination, and returning their bags was a holistic process. Kelleher was able to manage this customer experience at a personal level. If the plane had a mechanical problem, he would call you in advance. If a bag was misplaced, he would find it and drive it to your home. He also knew how he made his money because he was intimately involved with the cost and pricing levers. He saw immediately what worked and what did not work. He knew that operational excellence required a safe, clean plane that was on time—with its crew on board and ready to go—loaded with fuel and peanuts. He also knew that his suppliers would kill themselves to not let him down, and he treated them as an integral part of the Southwest family. Herb was the "system," and he had a great ability to sense what was happening and respond appropriately.

## Herb's Model

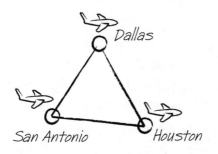

Given the size and scale of Southwest Airlines today (more than 500 aircraft), it is impossible to sense and respond in the same way the company did when it made its inaugural flight on June 18, 1971. However, the company's executives want the same feel and results. To achieve them, they are continuously simplifying and digitizing their core platform to drive out cost and maintain a high level of intimacy with customers, employees, and suppliers.

The physical events and processes that were connected in Herb's eyes and mind decades ago have been reconnected digitally. For example, if a gate is changed or an arrival time is delayed, everyone in the system is notified through a real-time infrastructure—the customers, gate agents, baggage handlers, websites, airport displays, caterers, mechanics, and crew. This real-time digital reconnection of processes can only be accomplished if your core is designed and built around the way work should be done, not the way you are functionally organized. I had the privilege to work with the Southwest Airline team, and they will be my case study for the HOW section of this book.

As we move from WHAT will we do to HOW will we go about doing it, I will begin to translate the business architecture into an applications and technology architecture. It is critical to approach this with big scenario themes—like changing the customer experience or a unified supply chain—which span functions and years, but to execute digestible projects like gate and boarding, kiosks, gate information display, flight information display, and virtual check-in. Plan big and implement in small chunks. That, when combined, will dramatically change the customer experience and productivity end to end. Watch for this pattern because it is the best formula for sustainable success, absorption, and affordability.

The next chapter will assume that you have developed a very strong and compelling WHY storyline and an inspiring and well-articulated destination for WHAT you will look like on the other side. Its focus will be on building a pathway to an affordable, properly sequenced, and paced execution plan or HOW.

# CHAPTER 5

WHY      WHAT      <u>HOW</u>      WHO

**THE HOW**

# HOW Will We Do It?

The HOW to change (HOW will we do it?). This is the pathway from your current model to your future model, and it is where the heavy lifting comes in for both the business and the IT organization. To be successful, the following three principles within the HOW (discussed in detail in this chapter) must be adhered to:

- **HOW Principle I:** Define and design a business, application, and technology blueprint and architecture before you begin investment and construction.
- **HOW Principle II:** Enforce a "Common Way" for development and quality engineering.
- **HOW Principle III:** Be disciplined in your approach to program and project management.

## 5A THE FRITO-LAY JOURNEY
# HOW We Did It

The idea of implementing a more flexible system at Frito-Lay—centralized at the core and decentralized at the customer edge—sounded great, but now the HOW became the overwhelming problem. HOW could we enable our business strategy with process, systems, and technology? That task fell to Leo Kiely—who ran sales and marketing at the time—Ron Rittenmeyer, and me. Ron was the perfect partner for me because he had run just about every field function there was, at every level.

I first met Ron in 1974 when I worked for IBM on the Frito-Lay account. He was the distribution manager at the Louisville, Kentucky plant. The plant had an IBM data-entry machine that was not functioning properly. I remember answering the phone and hearing him say that if someone from IBM did not fix this machine in the next few hours, then he was putting it out on the loading dock! There was no question in my mind that he was not kidding. Not a great start, but over the years we became good friends. Twelve years later, we were in charge of figuring out the HOW and the WHO for Frito-Lay's next 25 years.

At the heart of the HOW was the emerging handheld technology.

Implementing this customized segment-of-one strategy at the edge—while retaining our standardized manufacturing core— required flexible mobile technology so each route salesman would be able to tailor and communicate customer requirements daily in a granular form. This would allow manufacturing and distribution to aggregate the demand and continue to have long production runs.

Fortunately, we had actually started looking for and prototyping this handheld technology in 1981 to replace our aging OCR system, which was coming to the end of its technological life. The need for a technology-based solution was compelling. We had too many product line items for the salesmen to effectively record and manage on a manual basis. In addition, our customers hated the forms and their handwritten mistakes and corrections. Although I had support from within the organization, it was hard to make the financial case for a technology change to the board of directors. Like OCR a decade earlier, there was really no commercial solution readily available. So we kept prototyping and pushing internally. Although unwilling to make the big investment, the Frito-Lay culture always supported a passionate leader by providing a limited budget of experimentation dollars.

Eventually, as experienced a decade earlier, the real impetus to change came from the WHY and the WHAT. Wal-Mart started pushing us for consistent, everyday low pricing. Our entire system was geared for a twice-a-year price change and a set promotional calendar—Memorial Day, 4th of July, Labor Day, Back to School, Thanksgiving, and Christmas. All of this was preplanned and executed nationally, which enabled us to publish and distribute new forms to the 10,000 salesmen. Wal-Mart changed the game forever by using their supply chain power to gain special pricing and discounts from us. These changes required hard coding them into our systems and printing special forms that the route salesmen carried with them.

That was the beginning of the end, because soon Kroger, Tom Thumb, Safeway, 7-11, and all the other national and regional retailers wanted it their way, too. In fact, each one wanted pricing and promotions customized to the way they wanted to manage—not the way we had traditionally done things. Our limited ability to keep up with customized programming began to grind the organization to a halt.

Because of the way our systems were built, we depended on a programmer and printed forms to create unique pricing and promotions for each customer. We had to change the way our systems were architected so that sales and marketing had an applications workbench where they—not my programmers— could configure pricing and promotional calendars dynamically. Through our network and mobile technology, we needed to enable each salesman to profile their customers without having a separate form for each one, and to connect purchasing, manufacturing, and distribution to daily orders and sales.

The two streams of IT enablement—pushing for a technical replacement, and the need to operate a hybrid—came together in 1986, and we had our justification and design concepts in place. Now we needed a well-articulated IT HOW, but there were two big obstacles in our path.

The first obstacle was that it was the mid-1980s, well before the proliferation of Internet and mobile computing technologies. In fact, the first PCs were in the process of being implemented with Microsoft's DOS and IBM's OS/2. As a result, we had a number of technical problems to solve. For example, in-truck printer ink would freeze in Minnesota in the winter and melt in Texas in the summer. Networks were slow and expensive, and the core technology was large IBM mainframes.

The second obstacle was that a program of this magnitude typically called for a build and implementation that would take at least four years. My frustration was that we had been pushing on this from 1981 through 1985 with no real support from above. Now, no one could wait the four years we would need—until 1990—to build and implement the project. Everyone's opinion was that we in IT were late, slow, and bureaucratic. Fortunately, Ron understood the obstacles and was willing to help solve them rather than criticize. However, he was a tough hombre, and he insisted on a two-year implementation. He would take the responsibility to wire 10,000 trucks and train the salesmen, customers, and plants.

My job was to stop worrying about the timeframe and bring in the best and brightest—not just from my team, but also from our IT suppliers. We quickly centered up on IBM for the back-end, Fujitsu for the handheld technology, and AT&T for the network. I felt that getting the technical design, architecture, and blueprint in place was critical before we started to build. Since the technology was in such an early stage, miscalculation in design could not be overpowered with the kind of horsepower you could bring to bear in current networks and technologies. We particularly focused on database design and performance.

During my first four years as CIO, I built an eclectic team of older mainframe warriors, and mixed them with young fresh talent right out of college. More important, the culture was strong, confident, and willing to take prudent risk. Our teams signed up to get the new system developed and deployed in just two years.

## 5B

# HOW Will We Do It?

Once the broad outline of the plan is articulated, defining the HOW is extremely critical. It is the pathway for your people to execute the strategies you have developed. It should be a multiyear plan focused on implementation with expected timeframes, investments, and value creation. Unfortunately, this is where many executive teams drop the ball. The truth is that many enterprises have spent a fortune with consultancies to build their business/technology plans. Unfortunately, most end up becoming a book on a shelf instead of a real framework for organizational change. In my experience, this most often occurs for two reasons:

First, the executives and line-leadership teams have in many cases been passive participants in the strategy-formulation process, and have merely answered the questions that consultants ask. They have not personally and actively engaged in the process, there is little to no ownership on their parts, and as a result, the consultant-delivered roadmap may be threatening, naïve, or impractical—or all the above.

Second, even if the plan is spot on, a company's executives and board may have little confidence in their organization's ability to execute on time, on budget, and with realizable value. Many executive teams and boards believe that IT initiatives— particularly those that are multiyear and enterprise-wide—are as risky as an R&D or marketing investment, as opposed to relatively safe engineering or manufacturing efforts, which by nature have better-defined and measurable outcomes.

This fear is not completely unreasonable. The road of business is strewn with the wreckage of failed IT implementations. There have also been some superb successes. It's from both these successes and failures that I've built an execution framework (the HOW) that will enable you to dramatically reduce the randomness of your results while improving the odds of success.

Since this will be a multiyear investment, planning for IT is an activity that needs to be closely linked to the company's overall strategic imperatives and appropriately wide in aperture. It must also provide for long-term value creation and get delivered in meaningful chunks every six to nine months. Investments in IT should be supported by the underlying business value that they provide, and therefore, should be rationalized and prioritized based on the value that is generated to the entire enterprise—not just to a particular business segment.

Although most companies have fairly rigorous processes to rationalize non-IT investments (for example, distribution centers and plants), these same processes are not always applied to IT investments. IT is considered by many executives to be a mysterious black box—one that only the CIO understands and has the knowledge to unlock.

This is the blind spot.

Investments in information technology play a significant role in enabling a company to succeed in today's marketplace. It is important for executives to focus not only on the expected return generated from IT investments, but on the level of IT investments made on an annual basis. Companies that have wide swings in IT investment levels from year to year find it difficult to generate the desired economic returns and have lumpy execution.

The reason most enterprises manage this way is because they are much too fragmented in their approach or in the governance processes. Every leader of every function or business unit has their own opinion on how to optimize their investment and work. Some believe in IT and overspend, while others do not invest at all. What I've come to believe in my own career is that although democracy is a powerful way to manage a nation, it is probably the worst form of government when it comes to IT.

The approach to execution will be the toughest part of this book for a business leader to fully understand because IT execution has many technical items and nuances. This type of complex, multiyear, always-on development takes a great deal of technical skill and IT leadership. Therefore, I will try to keep this HOW section focused on what you should look for and expect your IT organization to be doing using three big principles. As you stay with it, you will soon recognize and pick up the patterns that are critical to success.

### HOW Principle I: Define and design a business, application and technology blueprint and architecture before you begin investment and construction.

Just because you bought the business plan (the WHY and WHAT) does not mean you have to write the entire check and wait a few years for the results. You should write a much smaller check and take the time up front to first ensure that your team has aligned the business architecture with the IT architecture and construction plan.

Unfortunately, most executives glaze over when the term architecture is mentioned. But before you decide to skip this section, let me use a simple analogy that makes the point.

If you were to build a house, before the construction teams got started you would have to work with an architect whose job it is to provide the electricians, carpenters, plumbers, and other tradespeople with some basic diagrams, material selections, and dimensions (architecture) for them to be able to deliver what you want, when you want it, and at a price you agreed to pay.

It is incredible to me just how many high-price-tag IT programs people are willing to invest in without the architecture first being described and aligned. As with my construction-project analogy, there are different layers of an IT architecture.

In the beginning stage of building a house, for example, you'll need a conceptual drawing followed by a floor plan and elevations which will give you a more visual look at what your new home will be like. Developing them is an interactive process that requires discussion and negotiation.

Maybe you would ideally like to build a 10,000-square-foot house, but you can only afford 5,000 right now. The house should therefore be designed and priced for what you need and can afford now, but expandable so the land and city ordinances can accommodate an eventual Phase II. Maybe you would like for it to be built entirely out of steel, but in reality, building mostly out of wood—with some strategically placed steel beams—is more than sufficient, and will reduce the cost. The same analogy would hold true for a subdivision or city plan. Where will you put the roads, utilities, shopping centers, and the rest of the infrastructure? I'll call this Layer 1. If you have ever built a house, you understand why this pre-work is so critical.

## Construction Artifacts

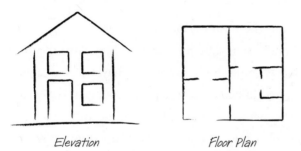

Elevation                Floor Plan

It helps you understand what you are buying, your investment risk tolerance, the level of quality you consider to be good enough, the timeline and sequencing you require—how you will phase it, where you will start, and more. You just cannot simply leave it to the electricians and the plumbers to make these decisions for you.

This is heavy lifting for the executive team—and particularly for the CIO and his or her team—and it is the translation bridge from the WHAT plan. The business architecture begins to break down the necessary investments into actionable, discrete pieces of work. It is a step that cannot be delegated or skipped, and most failed projects fail right here—before the project even begins. So devote the time and the right people to this important dialogue. This process should ideally take 90 days, co-owned by both IT and business leaders with a point of view on the most critical themes and programs in a multiyear cadence. Have the entire executive team look at the business architecture and formally approve or change it before allocating additional funding.

As we move from the business architecture to the supporting applications information and technical architecture, the role of IT leadership becomes more dominant. Layer 2 is all about the details required to construct a quality product at the "deal" price. In our home-construction example, it means turning the agreed-to floor plan into a construction plan. How would we break it down into construction sequencing? Foundation before roof. The layout of the wiring diagrams–the number of electrical outlets, how much power, the itemized cost to build—and more important, the cost to operate. Plumbers in first, because if we pour the concrete and forget the plumbing we will have to rip up the foundation. I could go on but you get the idea. This may require some re-estimation and re-timing but once done and reviewed, it should become the contract between the business and IT.

To be effective, this blueprinting work needs to be time-boxed to 90 to 180 days. This will help ensure that it does not become a science fair project. No one should be programming or buying servers while this is going on, because any changes made during this period will likely have to be thrown out once the architecture is defined. Obviously, this effort will have a lifespan, and much can be enhanced or refined over time as you get deeper into the effort. It needs enough energy and leadership to be directionally correct. Going slowly at first will allow you to go faster with higher quality and lower cost over time.

Make the effort as a leadership team. You can leverage consultancies but do not delegate this to anyone. By following this principle, you will dramatically reduce the risk, financial surprises, and re-work. Ignore this principle, however, and you will most likely get random results and very little business value out of all your investment and hard work. Unfortunately, the latter is the norm in many organizations, and in some cases the CIO gets replaced and the enterprise takes a write-off. In other cases, the projects are launched randomly. Even if these projects are completed, there are usually little-to-no realizable benefits— just extra IT costs—for isolated, one-off projects.

A solid multiyear plan, diligent process simplification, good architecture, proper leadership, and a disciplined approach will make your investment extremely durable and allow you to continuously evolve your business processes and technology and meet the demands of the marketplace change.

## HOW Principle II: Enforce a "Common Way" for development and quality engineering.

A quality-engineering methodology is as critical to IT execution as the sheet music is to a symphony. A symphony is made up of many instruments and individuals and—without the discipline of the composer's music and a strong leader—it will make nothing but noise.

So it is with an IT organization that is building high-quality enterprise solutions.

When I entered the IT profession in the 1960s—and up until the 1980s—most developers were trained to know enough about a variety of information technology, including hardware, software, network performance, and code development. We did our own analysis, design, coding and—in most cases—testing and production support. As the decades have gone by, IT has entered the era of specialization. While there are many pluses for this narrowing and deepening of skills, the one big downside is that it now takes a team of specialists to build a modern system.

The components of networks, virtualization of hardware, operating systems, and security have become so complex in this global, always-on world that it takes a team of specialists to build large, complex systems. To know when to bring these specialists into the development process requires that you have a well-articulated, quality-engineering methodology and leaders who buy in and enforce it in a thoughtful way.

In large transformational work, there are also many changes to business processes, organization, structures, incentives, culture, and financials that must be managed and harmonized as systems are built and deployed. The overall methodology must include business workstreams that are integrated with the systems development lifecycle. In the case of the Frito-Lay handheld project, for example, this included everything from wiring the route trucks, to changing sales processes, creating new customer-billing systems, and setting up repair depots and staging spares—all of which had to be planned and executed in lockstep with the systems development lifecycle.

Most organizations have selected a development methodology, but its enforcement often takes one of two ineffective paths. The first is the optional one, where teams can choose to follow it or not. The second is to make the development methodology so rigid—and to enforce it with such an overbearing bureaucracy—that it will grind development to a snail's pace. You cannot let either of those approaches establish your operating culture. You must establish clear roles and responsibilities between the business and IT, and among the various IT groups. I'll discuss this further in the Leadership and Culture section of the WHO Principles. But for now let's focus on the minimal mechanics of methodology and release planning in a modern development environment.

As in my symphony analogy, if you start with a weak piece of music, the overall experience will not be a good one, regardless of the quality of the musicians. The same is true with a poorly constructed IT plan. To have a quality, well-engineered IT delivery, you must start with a thoughtful, well-paced, and integrated program/project release plan built around a well-understood, phased, and tollgated cadence.

The **release plan** approach to strategic multiyear projects is key to delivering large enterprise initiatives. It must:

- Group new major applications, enhancements, and requisite infrastructure deliveries that fit within a given timeframe. Releases may be from three to twelve months apart (usually six months). Make sure the business workstreams are included and synchronized.
- Provide a consistent way of managing delivery of software, function, and organizational change to the business.

- Optimize testing resources with end-to-end use cases or real business scenarios.
- Provide rally points for the development, infrastructure, business partners, and support organizations to converge at specified tollgates.

The tollgates are rally points where key members from each team meet to communicate and resolve issues of design, timing, or resources. This is critical because in an airline, for example, a major release may include projects and integration with flight operations, reservations, baggage handling, maintenance development teams, and support from the infrastructure engineering, suppliers, and business teams. All of these constituencies would have components or subassemblies that had to be designed and delivered together. Tollgates need to be touch points built around a phased methodology.

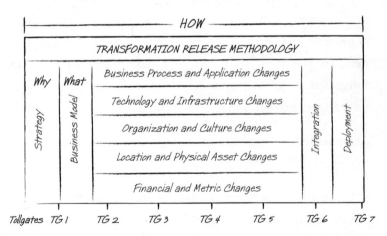

Any brand of methodology that is selected will include the following phases or tollgates:

- Phase 1: Initiation. The project team defines the project request and assesses the business impact. The outcomes identify basic information about the project and work breakdown structures, and determine the path and deliverables for the project.

- Phase 2: Requirements. The focus of this phase is on business processes and major information needs. Current and proposed processes are identified and documented. A set of detailed functional requirements is delivered.
- Phase 3: Design. The functional requirements are translated into an application design with technical specifications. The application's architecture is defined.
- Phase 4: Construction. The application is built (assembled, coded, and/or configured). This phase includes the unit testing of the application's components.
- Phase 5: System Testing. This phase includes testing of the application's components together. Functionality testing is conducted using test scenarios developed from the use cases developed in the requirements and design phases.
- Phase 6: Integration and Acceptance Testing. This phase includes testing the application with all of its linkages in a production-like environment. This testing is much more controlled and—if the project is included in a multiyear plan—it includes the entire release. Performance and regression testing are also completed in this phase. Thorough testing helps to ensure quality software.
- Phase 7: Implementation & Deployment. This phase includes pilot implementations, rolling deployments, and installations. Training and monitoring are included.
- Phase 8: Support. This is the phase that completes the project and the application is rolled into the normal support framework. Learnings are documented and project deliverables are archived as appropriate.

Throughout the development cycle, the business and IT teams must play an active role. However, at each phase, who leads and who supports alternates. For example, Phases 1 and 2—Initiation and Requirements—are the domain of the business with IT questioning, modeling, and structuring the artifacts. During Phases 3 and 4—Design and Construction— the roles and responsibilities flip. Roles and responsibilities are shared equally during Phases 5 and 6—System Testing and Integration and Acceptance Testing. The business leads Phase 7—Implementation and Deployment. Finally, IT leads Phase 8—Support. Those best practices are seldom followed, but are in my opinion the only kind of partnership that can be productive and consistently deliver quality on time and on budget.

## Development Pipeline

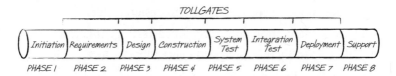

The discipline of the tollgates and methodology must be the vehicle that brings the right specialist in at the right time. After a self-service application to sell airline tickets or check people into a flight has been implemented, it is too late to bring in the security expert or the network engineer to help with a security or response-time problem. It needs to be specific for this class of application during the design phase when you need to bring these types of skills in to help and sign off on the development team. This is why I believe the methodology combined with an accountable leadership team are the difference between great and affordable IT, and terrible and expensive IT.

If done properly, the focus should be on required deliverables—not on checking boxes. Each phase of the methodology includes a required set of deliverables and activities. These are published and used in the phase checkpoints or tollgate activities. Critical to the success of the methodology are the development environments, tools, and templates. Deliverable templates, best practices, and tools guide the developer through the work. As with any good methodology, the tools and templates should enable the development teams and business owners to communicate and collaborate with one another in a totally transparent way. They do not provide the thought, analysis, and creativity that are required to develop sound applications.

The tools and templates have to provide flexibility for the experienced developer, yet enough structure for the less-experienced developer. There should be a balance based on the strengths of each organization. The particular brand of methodology you select is not as important as narrowing it to a common one for the enterprise, and then thoughtfully applying it to your own environment. I would like to emphasize that this methodology is meant to be enterprise-wide, including business, engineering, and operations—not just for the development teams. It should include progress to plan, quality metrics, resource consumption, financing, etc. A poorly engineered, always-on modern system can be an order of magnitude more costly if it is not well designed, with run costs and quality built in.

### HOW Principle III: Be disciplined in your approach to program and project management.

The architecture in HOW Principle I, and the quality engineering in HOW Principle II, are basic structural building blocks. HOW Principle III gives the first two principles both life and motion.

Don't get me wrong—the first two principles are both critical processes and structures, but the way you manage them together is the thing that will give you results.

Almost every enterprise either under-manages or over-manages projects because they believe their managers will manage well, or because they do not think they can be trusted to be disciplined.

The first example is a laissez faire approach where leaders hope good things happen through the entire process of integration with other applications and infrastructure. The most prevalent result of this approach is cost, quality, and on-time delivery problems. The second example is an upside-down bureaucracy where your developers and line managers are being controlled by—and have to answer to—a layer of project managers and checkers that adds no business or technical value to the dialogue. When they take over your organization, the result is less risk, but cost, speed, and innovation are all casualties.

The most successful answer from top-performing IT organizations is to build a culture of delivery. In a delivery culture, hands-on managers lead their teams. Project administrators, human resource generalists, and financial analysts support the teams during the lifecycle of a project. They do not control the agenda, nor are they accountable for the outcomes. Top-tier technicians, architects, and leaders participate in the tollgate sessions and project reviews. These are meant to be productive, working meetings that are non-punitive and owned by the leaders of the organization.

The project-review process is meant to be self-disciplining. There should be no methodology police nor process cops. The value of the meetings should become evident to the project teams. What should also be evident to the organization is that the top technical and business leaders are driving the process. The reviews are not only control checkpoints but also learning experiences for project teams. Both the reviews and the designs improve over time. Project teams begin to develop shared understandings of expectations and become trusting so that news—whether good or bad—flows unfettered from the teams to the leadership.

Watch out for bureaucracy. The leadership team sets the tone of an IT organization. If leaders are entrenched in paperwork, presentations, reviews, bureaucracy, and formality, chances are the development teams will be also. I've found that the degree of formality and rigidity should be related to the complexity and risk of the business. Air traffic control and credit card processing are two extreme examples where software development cannot be as fluid as, for example, a marketing or business-intelligence project.

Setting a cadence for reviews, meetings, and tollgates helps to establish participation and a manageable level of calendar planning across the IT organization.

- Pick a day of the week that is regularly held for staff meetings, at whatever level. This helps to link the communication pipeline down through the organization.
- A day-a-week focus on project updates, reviews, and tollgates (Governance Day) time boxes the productivity drain of preparation and participation in project management-related activities for the development and leadership teams.

The other days of the week should be dedicated to real work. Build your leadership team with players who are solutions focused and tough minded, but supportive and people oriented.

The multiyear plan should set common goals for the teams and individuals to understand that they cannot be successful if the organization is not successful. The isolated and competitive spirit needs to be replaced with an interdependent, resilient, and trusting mindset. Modern enterprise development is a collaborative team sport.

In addition, applications maintenance and support teams play key roles in an IT organization. They keep the wheels on the businesses, ensuring that day-to-day applications run efficiently. They're the front line of the organization and can build or tear down IT credibility. They also provide integration and functional knowledge. Applications quality will be improved by involving these support technicians in the requirements, design, and testing of new applications. Don't separate your maintenance and development teams from one another. Too many enterprises see maintenance as a low-level job that can be isolated to another organization. Ideally, they should work for the same leadership team—even in cases where it is outsourced.

This program-management system should drive consistent behaviors and provide a process for all IT to participate throughout the lifecycle. On the business side, the methodology creates a forum for management review, participation, and the sharing of risk.

Using this principle-based approach to development creates a disciplined HOW to do the work that takes IT from a craft to a profession. You cannot get excellence in IT without a disciplined, organized, and consistent approach—no matter how much technical talent you have. At Southwest Airlines this approach became known as the SWA Way.

As a business leader, this is probably more information that you need. However, having a sense of how your IT group does its work is a leading indicator of execution success.

The key reason for the early focus on the HOW is that IT execution has, in general, been extremely sporadic. According to an IDC[5] study of IT projects reported several years ago:

- 30 percent are cancelled before completion
- 50 percent cost 200 percent of the original estimate
- 10 percent are completed on time and on budget
- 200 percent is the average time overrun of the original estimate

As important as execution statistics are, the reality is that most software—even when executed on time and budget—was either built poorly or did not deliver the expected business value. After embracing the three HOW principles, organizations have turned these statistics around—making dramatic and long-lasting improvement.

The quality of the HOW is inextricably linked to the quality of the WHO. I describe why talent matters, why leadership matters, and why culture matters to successful IT-enabled modernization in Chapter 6.

[5] IDC

## 5C CASE STUDY
# Southwest Airlines

Southwest Airlines is a compelling example of a corporation that has moved from spotty IT execution—often with frustrating results—to dependable and credible functioning. They did this by adopting our HOW Principles a few years ago:

HOW Principle I: Define and design a business, application and technology blueprint and architecture before you begin investment and construction.

HOW Principle II: Enforce a "Common Way" for development and quality engineering.

HOW Principle III: Be disciplined in your approach to program and project management.

Although this section is about HOW, it is important to understand the WHY and the WHAT of Southwest Airlines. Throughout the framework, context is critical because of the interdependence of the change planks.

Immediately following the 9/11 terrorist attacks, the airline business was turned on its head. The reticence of many Americans to fly in the aftermath of the attacks crippled the industry for more than a year. By 2003, however, Southwest Airlines' business was back. In the meantime, the productivity that is core to Southwest's low-cost value proposition had begun to show signs of eroding. Several things had changed that were somewhat masked by the downturn.

For one, Southwest's beautifully simple first-come, first-served boarding process had to embrace a much more restrictive set of airport security rules. The company was required to upgrade its highly efficient boarding pass system with preprinted names and positive identification. That began to change its low-tech, high-touch approach as security and national policy intruded on the customer experience. In addition to having a direct impact on customers, these changes added complexity, which cascaded throughout the system and impacted productivity.

Herb Kelleher, Southwest's executive chairman (at the time) and co-founder, had a radically simple vision of what an airline should be. Fly clean, reliable airplanes from one underserved city to another, and have fun doing it. Standardize everything so that you can quickly and easily interchange people, planes, and equipment when there is a problem, and create a value proposition around low cost with a consistent experience. Keep it low tech. Keep it intimate. Above all, keep it simple. No assigned seating, no frills, on-time arrivals, and great customer service. Southwest's approach was so simple and basic. And it was so efficient, convenient and reliable that many of the airline's customers bought tickets right at the airport on the day of travel.

Another change in Southwest's business environment concurrent with the domestic deregulation of the industry in 1978 was that the airline began to grow its route structures outside the Southwestern U.S. to the East and West Coasts. As a result, the company introduced new layers of complexity into its business. It had to deal with an operation with geometrically more variables such as inclement weather and air traffic control logjams—none of which they had much control of. On-time arrivals and departures—a Southwest cornerstone—were more difficult to achieve, and it was showing up in the airline's productivity.

Another trademark of this extremely successful airline was its high levels of customer service. In its earlier years, everything was done with common processes and an entire fleet of aircraft comprised of just one manufacturer and model—the Boeing 737. The 737 was the epitome of interchangeability, and so was everything else in the company. Everything, that is, except IT. Because Southwest's business model was so simple and disciplined, Herb and team pretty much ignored IT for many years. This was enabled by the company's simple hands-on-intimacy model that required very little IT, while compiling the best record of continuous profitability and job security in the history of the airline industry.

That made sense for many years because IT is required only if you have scale or complexity. Southwest did not even have an

IT department as late as the mid-1990s—each function within the company was empowered to use computers if they needed to. Without an overall company business/technology plan, managers were given free rein to create a series of freestanding systems that supported only their organization. Moreover, Southwest also went slow on IT in anticipation that the rapidity of IT improvements would increase power and flexibility and reduce cost at a rapid rate.

Scale came to Southwest Airlines, however, as the company approached and then exceeded 500 planes within its fleet. Complexity was brought to the airline when it added long haul flights to its commuter service, bringing with them the increased baggage for vacationers, versus the carry-ons that commuters favored. The thick icing on this change cake was the addition of tighter regulations by Homeland Security and the FAA in the post-9/11 world.

Gary Kelly—then-CFO, now current chairman & CEO— recognized that the systems, processes, and technology that were adequate for the company's first three decades were becoming a barrier to the airline's expansion plans. Low cost, high customer satisfaction was Southwest's brand, and the company would be under huge pressure from the competition if this brand could not be maintained. He also saw the company's IT investment escalating dramatically as each function accelerated spending to solve its problems.

In 2002, Gary and I discussed the issues and the options, and we agreed that even though Southwest could no longer control all of the variables that impacted their business proposition, they could more consistently manage the outcomes through more effective, IT-enabled end-to-end process management.

Most of these disconnected, "stovepiped" systems grew organically—one good idea at a time. Many were done well but some were not, depending on the way IT was managed and governed by each function head. Gary, Herb, and then-president Colleen Barrett caught on very quickly, and they did so because they could see that the principles that they had rigorously adhered to in their business model and the way they managed the now crucial IT assets were sharply opposite. They were able to see the contradiction.

| Business Model | IT Model |
|---|---|
| Every aircraft was a 737 | Whatever technology made sense at the time |
| Common ways of operating | Every group did IT their own way |
| Simplicity was foundational | Complexity was the norm |
| Operational intensity and accountability at every level | Low accountability for business results |

Functional excellence was imbedded deep in the Southwest culture, and that was reflected in the "stovepipe" nature of the IT systems. Each function optimized IT cost and quality. However, it's in the seams between flight operations, maintenance, baggage handling, and so forth where overall cost and quality are achieved. In many cases, fairly average functional systems that are integrated will outperform highly optimized but isolated components. This is particularly true in an airline.

## *Functional - Stovepipe*
## *Internal Focus*

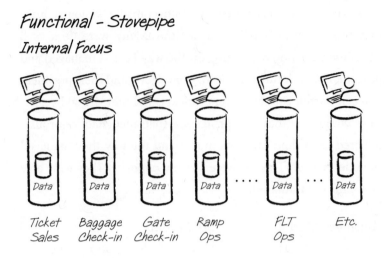

| Ticket Sales | Baggage Check-in | Gate Check-in | Ramp Ops | FLT Ops | Etc. |

For example, if a plane was late—necessitating a gate change or passenger rebooking or baggage transfer—there was no way to quickly and easily communicate this news from one function or system to another. To maintain its traditionally high levels of service in the face of increasing inefficiencies, Southwest began to cover systems shortfalls with people power. Expediting between functions was being done by a growing layer of staff, and this approach was insidiously eating into the company's productivity, cost structure, and profit.

Most businesses are geared for regular operations. An airline system is different—it needs to be geared for irregular operations. Otherwise, the slightest problem with weather, equipment, crews, or a variety of other factors can cause service to crumble like a house of cards. As a result, the value of intersystem communications becomes more important than the quality of any one application. The general rule is that you lose bags not because of a poor baggage handling system, but because the baggage system is disconnected from the flight ops and passenger systems.

Southwest Airlines' IT systems needed to be modernized to support this new expanded and more complex world. The company's leadership team knew WHY they had to change—to prevent the erosion of productivity that would eventually break Southwest's low-cost model—and they were willing to make the required investments. WHAT they had to do was to focus on the customer's end-to-end experience from outside in, not functional inside-out improvements. The big shift in WHAT they needed to do was to focus their systems and processes on irregular operations and become really great at recovering, in addition to preventing. That meant connecting all functions to what was called the "heartbeat."

## Customer Focused – End to End

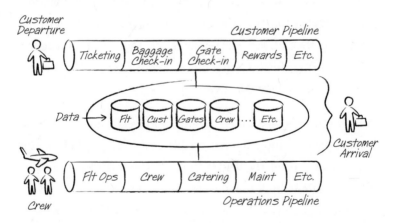

When I was the CIO at Delta Air Lines, this was what we called the Delta Digital Nervous System.[6] Its design was to capture events from all transactions to the central database and publish any irregularities to the appropriate system for handling. For example, if a New York-bound flight was departing late because of a snowstorm, everyone who would be affected downstream by the late flight would be notified, including the passengers who

[6] MIT Case Study

would miss their connecting flights in Dallas, baggage transfers, rebooking, and others. This would enable improved service, maintain low cost, and be infinitely scalable.

The WHAT was about the business architecture and processes, or the way the enterprise needed to operate in the future state to maintain the highly reliable, low-cost model.

This front-end work was done well at Southwest Airlines, and it proved to be well worth it. The leaders of all Southwest's major functions agreed that the build sequencing should be focused on those systems that actually touched the customers. That agreement then logically led the executive team to identify the gate and boarding systems as the initial target—or Release 1—of the multiyear plan. The gate systems and the boarding process touch every customer at the most critical moment. Everything comes together at the gate—planes, customers, maintenance, crews, catering, fueling, and more. Every function has to put forth effort to make it effective.

The big question was: HOW could Southwest count on a more dependable execution at a reasonable cost from their IT group? Tom Nealon, one of The Feld Group CIOs, and Jan Marshall, one of our development leaders, were assigned to help Gary and his team create the SWA Way for managing and delivering systems using our time-proven principles:

HOW Principle I: Define and design a business, application, and technology blueprint and architecture before you begin investment and construction.

HOW Principle II: Enforce a "Common Way" for development and quality engineering.

HOW Principle III: Be disciplined in your approach to program and project management.

The SWA Way consisted of a common methodology, a program/project management system, technical architecture design, inter-systems communication highway or integration fabric, common data names and terminology, hardware and software platforms, and security frameworks. Although it required a lot of upfront work and was time consuming, it was at the heart of successful execution.

## Making the Planned Tollgates Useful

Having established the SWA Way created a playbook for all teams providing a forum for an overt decision to move on to the next phase—or to spend more time getting it right. Southwest Airlines used tollgating more diligently than any of our other clients.

These sessions included senior and technical leadership from the business, application development, common services, and operations groups. Each functional leader brought the appropriate experts to each session based on the subject or phase to be covered. The primary leadership role would shift depending on phase. For example, the VP of operations chaired any production-readiness review session. This ensured the highest level of buy-in possible by the responsible leaders.

There are questions that the project teams came prepared to answer at each tollgate, independent of the project phase:

| Topic Details | Schedule |
| --- | --- |
| | Current status to project plan (schedule variance) |
| | Dependencies (other development projects, common services, external) |
| | Scope |
| | Release plan |
| | Any reductions or additions to scope |
| | Risks/new risks |
| | Mitigation plans |
| | Outstanding Issues |
| | Staffing (current staff and planned additions) |
| | Financial (current status of financial plan and budget variance status) |
| | Communications (external groups involved to this point in the project) |
| Tollgate Outcome | Approval or sign off on the completed phase |
| | Commitment on approach and resources for the next phase |
| | Concurrence on the project schedule and milestones |
| | Approval or sign off for the next phase |
| | Action plans to address project concerns or issues |

As you can see, implementing a collaborative, modern development environment is very heavy on methodology, tools, processes and artifacts. However, to make it real requires a strong WHO, because talent, leadership, and culture all really matter. The final section will be devoted to getting the organization and governance right.

# CHAPTER 6

**THE WHO**

# WHO Will Lead and Manage the Change?

The WHO (WHO will lead and manage the change?) This is the last plank in the platform. You will see my personal bias revealed in this chapter because, although I believe all of the planks are important, the human aspect makes the real difference! This chapter outlines the key human-resource principles required for sustained successes, including:

- WHO Principle I: Organization Matters
- WHO Principle II: Leadership Matters
- WHO Principle III: Culture Matters
- WHO Principle IV: Performance Matters

All of these human-resource principles matter whether you outsource, smartsource, or go it alone.

## 6A THE FRITO-LAY JOURNEY
# WHO Led the Change

The critical WHO of talent, culture, structures, and decision rights is where PepsiCo and Frito-Lay really shined. A leader-led, risk-oriented culture had been built up over the years from Herman Lay and Don Kendall, to Andy Pearson, Wayne Calloway, Mike Jordan, and Roger Enrico. People were trained, rewarded, and supported for taking prudent risks that had the potential to lead to business value. We were at our best when we were out on a limb. Ron Rittenmeyer and I were certainly there in 1986, but we never thought about failing. At worst, we might be a little late, but we would never fail. More important, the corporate culture was so deep that the bulk of the 10,000 salesmen and all of our plant and field operations leaders embraced change.

With that wind at our backs—and the support of the executive team—we signed up for the two years. As it turned out, our new system was actually fully deployed in less than two years, but we had many problems at first. Once we got through the development, we had to put the project on hold in Minneapolis and Dallas until we worked out the bugs. But when we got through that, Ron and his field teams flew through the route truck installations, training, and the sales force change program. In fact, toward the end we deployed nearly 2,000 handhelds in just one month. The completion of the deployment was so stunningly abrupt that we had not begun to think about the celebration party.

However, let me go back to 1981, when Wayne Calloway hired me to run the IT organization. Everything I said about leader led, risk oriented, and talent rich applied to all of Frito-Lay. That is, except for the IT organization. In fact, that was the major part of his initial discussion with me. Why was the IT organization and culture so different from the rest of the company? Was it different because by its technical nature it had to be, or because people saw their careers being in the IT profession instead of in the company? Can a snack-food company attract and retain top IT talent? Can people move in and out of IT as they do in marketing, planning, manufacturing, and other functions? Will top performers be willing to move from one division of PepsiCo to another or are they Dallas-only residents?

It was interesting to me that while most companies assume all the above to be true, Calloway and team had a hard time accepting it. They believed that people were people and were motivated by the same things: opportunity, passion for the work, camaraderie, and a sense of belonging and contributing. I agreed with

Calloway—not because he was the CEO, but because I came up through the systems engineering ranks and had a strong belief in the Pygmalion effect. Treat me like a transient worker and I will become one. However, treat me like a family member, have high expectations, hold me accountable for my contributions, and reward me appropriately, and I will make the company my passion like everyone else.

The key message is this: Do not treat IT folks any different than you treat people in any other profession.

With that in mind, we proceeded to adopt all of the PepsiCo leadership-development processes: recruiting, performance management, talent management, selection, and succession planning. Recruiting was focused on bringing in the best athletes as opposed to hiring to a specific job slot. We had a good mix of college recruits with a few spotted professional hires. We set up recruiting teams of three people each—one to bear down on technical competence, one to make sure we had a strong cultural affinity, and one to sell the applicant on joining us. We had five teams of three—all personally picked by my direct reports and me. This process included a meeting with me and my team at the end of each recruiting day while the interviews were fresh in everyone's mind. If there was any hesitation, we would pass on the applicant. Our belief was that a mistake here was a gift that would keep on giving.

Once people were recruited, we were diligent about their first assignment. It was critical to get the person oriented and mentored into the system by positive role models. Through a formal performance-planning-and-feedback system, our expectations were clearly communicated. Feedback to our people was continuous, but required four times a year—not just on the annual corporate cycle. That would give the individual a chance to improve as opposed to a once-a-year pass/fail call.

We were also serious about differentiating performance and, therefore, compensation. To that end, we constantly calibrated job categories and levels across the organization. We wanted to level off the managers who were hard graders from those who were easy graders. As part of the calibration session, we talked not just about performance, but also potential. I was constantly looking for my next leaders, both technical and managerial. It is possible and even probable that two people can perform at a very high level, but one has a lot more growth potential than the other. Having an eye for that kind of talent with upside was a hallmark of the PepsiCo system. It was a growth company that believed our future potential would be limited only by our supply of leadership talent. Much of my value to the company as a senior executive was as much about me being a net supplier of talent as it was about my project delivery.

Because of that dynamic, building a strong bench of talent and having depth at every position was a huge part of the leadership culture. The flip side of that equation was washing out the weaker, lower-potential players to create headroom and opportunity for the up-and-coming leaders. That kept the system vibrant.

Character, results orientation, and commitment to the team—mixed with the intellectual integrity and courage to disagree—were all pervasive parts of our culture. Our meetings actually took place in the meetings, not afterwards in the halls. Once you had your say and you broke the huddle, everyone was committed.

As you can see, this kind of human resource management system is time consuming. I would guess from 1981 to 1985 my leaders and I spent at least one-third of our time working on the organization. By the 1985–1986 timeframe, we had a deep bench of talent and a strong culture that paid huge dividends because we helped shaped the WHY change, WHAT to change, and HOW to go about it. And just as important, we now had also developed a respected team of highly talented people that were committed and capable of pulling off such a complex, risky, and time-compressed change program. The rest is well-documented history of another 20-plus years of growth and innovation.[7]

---

[7] Harvard Business School Case Study Frito-Lay Inc.: A Strategic Transition (Consolidated) July, 1993

## 6B PEPSICO/FRITO-LAY

# WHO Will Lead and Manage the Change?

Given a compelling, well-articulated WHY, a clearly defined WHAT, and a pathway to execution (HOW), whether or not you'll successfully deliver at all gets down to how you lead and govern the enterprise.

No matter how well done the plan or how well intentioned the organization, there will be a constant battle between short-term and long-term needs and function or business-unit pressures versus the enterprise's need to change. How the resources get allocated—and who gets to decide—is the most critical contribution the executive team can make to ensure success. The team with the best talent, in the right structure, and with clear decision rights and accountability will almost always win.

Like most things, legislating rules from the corner office will only take you so far. A strong and sustained leadership culture—from the top of the organization to the front line—is the only way to muster the energy for sustainable and systemic change. Although I describe the needed governance structure and processes in this chapter, I will primarily focus on the leadership, accountability, and performance dimensions.

I was fortunate to spend most of my formative business career at PepsiCo, which was one of the great leadership machines of the '70s, '80s, and '90s. It was a leader-led company where performance mattered. It took risks with people. Not just up or out, but laterally—proactively moving people from function to function, division to division, and country to country. A 35-year-old PepsiCo leader out of a top school had enough movement and mentoring under his or her belt to have the broad perspective and general management skills of a 55-year-old executive in many other firms.

Weak leaders were flushed out of the organization early. When combined with our strong and consistent growth, this constantly created opportunities for extraordinary people. It was a culture of big ideas backed up with flawless execution—more led by role models than by management training—and it was supported by a "batting-average" risk tolerance. All of this created within PepsiCo an optimism that was tough minded, and a confidence that was balanced with humility.

When I left to form my own CIO-for-hire company in 1992, I actually thought that every organization was like that. I was therefore quite surprised when I would walk into large organizations that were bureaucratic, over managed and under led, risk averse, and entitled. I found this particularly curious because the people in these dysfunctional organizations were bright, hard working, good at what they did, and extremely committed.

So what was missing?

What was missing was leadership development and perspective. Many managers had been in the same job—doing more or less the same thing—for 15 to 20 years or longer. There was little to no differentiation of performance between low performers and high performers. The cultures were designed to enable managers to hold onto their best employees, so there was little movement and few opportunities for employees to broaden their experience. As a result, the confidence to take a risk was almost nonexistent.

Seeing this problem of the human condition in these organizations, I rapidly came to believe that it was much easier to create the vision and strategy of the WHY, get the funding and support of the WHAT, and shape the artifacts and roadmaps of the HOW, than it was going to be to get a leadership team within the business and IT groups to execute the programs. At PepsiCo/ Frito Lay, I knew that if I got the plan and the money approved, we had a leadership team in place with skills. They could inspire their staff to want to get up in the morning and go to work. My job was to plan the celebration and make sure people did not have to kill themselves getting the job done.

If there's one thing I've learned over the years, it's that spending most of your time as a leader on the talent dimension is the difference between winning and losing at this sport. Every organization that gets IT right is good at this dimension.

The WHO can be summarized by four key principles that I explore in detail in the balance of this chapter:

- Organization Matters
- Leadership Matters
- Culture Matters
- Performance Matters

## WHO Principle I: Organization Matters

Some organizations are so complex that even good athletes cannot play the game well—no matter how hard they try. There are so many handoffs that these organizations are required to put massive groups in place to manage the seams. The inevitable result is a huge bureaucracy where there are more people watching, facilitating, measuring, or criticizing than there are people actually doing the work.

One IT organization that I led for a few years had 2,500 people when we started, but only 500 were actually doing development, maintenance, and operating tasks. The other 2,000 men and women were in management and support roles. That's not to say you do not need project offices and management and support organizations like finance, human resources, and communications—you do—but the ratio was upside down.

I put in place a simple structure with clear roles and responsibilities, reasonable spans and layers, and line-led accountability. This enabled us to change the ratio of doers to supporters within our organization from 80:20 overhead to 20:80—reducing the cost structure and getting more output more quickly. It also had the positive byproduct of requiring much less effort because the friction points and frustration were reduced. The dynamic with business users was fundamentally changed because it put them directly in touch with their development team—not some functional group that acted as a go-between.

Since organization matters, I am a strong believer in the following set of governing principles built around simplicity and de-layering:

**Process driven development teams.** The best and most-effective governance structure is one that is process aligned, not necessarily aligned to the way the business is organized. By that I mean systems have got to be built the way work (processes) of the enterprise is performed, not adapted to the management and politics of the organization. Organizational structures are crafted certain ways for many reasons—some thoughtful, some not so thoughtful—and they are an ever-changing kaleidoscope based on the current leadership team.

The way you load and unload passengers in an airline, or the way you track shipments or bill customers in a freight business, are very durable processes that do not care how you are organized. They must be continually simplified, re-engineered, and automated and that is what systems development should be focused on.

In most enterprises, there are seldom more than four major processes (for example: customer, operations, product marketing, and back office). IT organizations should be structured around these four, or in some cases five, development groups. These groups should be entrusted with cradle-to-grave responsibility—including design, code, test, and support—and each group should be under a strong development leader who can line up with the business leaders.

This strong development leader's turf may include many sub-functions that relate to customer experience. His or her job, and the job of the team, is to smooth out the seams that a customer often feels transitioning between different parts of the organization, and deliver a superior end-to-end experience. In the best-run companies, each process director or vice president would have no more than six to ten leaders—one over each sub-function—and each of those leaders should have teams of no more than 60–100 developers. Front-line development managers should have an eight-to-twelve-person team. The exact numbers would vary based on the size of the organization.

This kind of structure has a number of advantages.

- From the business perspective it is fairly stable, there is end-user intimacy and named accountability, it concentrates on workflows and processes, and it creates a knowledgeable team.
- From the developer's perspective it is empowering to be part of a team doing important work for the business and not just writing or supporting systems, and the spans and layers give them enough elbow room to get their work done but enough hands-on management contact to get real-time feedback.

Over the years, systems work has become so specialized and complex that—much like the medical profession—very few people can know the whole patient, or in the case of IT, all facets of technology. There was a time when a good developer knew enough about business, data-management design, coding, network response time, operating systems, and hardware to get the job done. No one person can know everything in this increasingly complex world, and this is the key reason why project teams and IT organizations have grown so large, with so many handoffs and so much overhead.

This can and must be moderated by these development teams so that even though one person cannot have all of these skills, the team can. This becomes much more effective when individuals are cross-trained. While they will not be experts in the different areas outside those within their immediate focus, they will know enough about a variety of things to be, if not totally capable, at least effective.

For example, every developer should be well schooled in project management. Over the years, project management has become a profession unto itself. You can dramatically reduce the number of project managers if your developers are capable of project management.

**Common-services team.** In addition to these process-driven development teams, there is one other critical development group, and that is the fifth—or common-services—team. One of the most productive ways to improve quality and cycle time—and reduce cost—is to simply write less code. The common-services team's primary mission is to design and build component code and frameworks that all other development teams can re-use. They should also provide all of the inter-systems communications and messaging that is so critical to seamless end-to-end operations that are required in this 21st century commerce model. Since most of the development teams will be integrating package software, legacy code, and custom services, they will need overarching portal, security, data, messaging, and other key frameworks and platforms so when a customer goes to your website or a driver picks up a shipment, it both feels and acts seamlessly.

**World-class operations team.** Finally, you need a world-class operations team because once you are operating in real time, you cannot afford to ever go down. Always on means always on. Not on every day except Sunday or 23 hours a day or not on Christmas Eve. It means ALWAYS ON. The skill and collaborative capability of the leaders of this group are paramount to success. They need to engage the development teams early and often. They need to deeply understand the technology and operating discipline. Their systems engineering teams need to understand performance, asset utilization, security, resilience, and more. The front-line operators need to have a real sense of urgency, customer service, and professional commitment to get the job done—regardless of the circumstance. Equipment does break, hackers do try to gain entry, oceanic cables are accidentally cut.

They must plan for all of this and keep things running.

## Simple, Accountable IT Structure
### Business Systems Development Teams

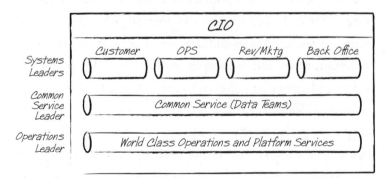

What I've just described is an organization that is well managed and well led. I have not really focused on whether it is insourced or outsourced because this book is about leadership. It is not about the particular software or hardware products, or consulting, or outsourced services you can acquire. Most IT organizations do not fully go it alone anymore. The products and services offered by specialized suppliers are often compelling. However, the feeling of team and teamwork and organizing principles transcends organizational and company boundaries. Organizations that treat their suppliers as partners—that bring them in close, and expect them to perform as part of the team—get much better results that those that wring them out in a procurement bid and treat them as vendor-contractors.

Get your organization simple and right, and you are on your way to success. Get it complex and wrong, and you will never meet the enterprise's expectations, nor its full potential. Given the stakes and tasks, the next principle, which focuses on leadership and culture, is the differentiator. It can make or break your efforts.

## WHO Principle II: Leadership Matters

I've just described an organization structure for IT that requires 50–100 leaders depending on the size of your organization. In order to win at these kinds of change programs, the business needs a comparable number. To sustain a multiyear transformation, most large companies require 100–200 leaders who are capable and bought in. They must be identified, recruited, trained, and incentivized.

Over the years, I have come to realize there are no perfect leaders, but there are great leadership teams. Generally, a leader will be really great at a few things, okay at a few others and often miserable at a few other things. I've spent a lot of time and energy recruiting, selecting, and developing leaders for this profession because it is the one thing—more than anything else—that determines success.

The way most leaders progress through their careers is by the implicit judgment of their manager. Some managers have an excellent eye for talent, while others do not. The managers who are skilled at selecting good leaders are not necessarily themselves skilled at developing good leaders. I felt early on that we needed leaders at all levels, and I was not willing to let Darwin's process of natural selection prevail. I have therefore passionately continued to enhance and evolve my early leadership experiences in a very explicit way.

I've written a number of articles about this—and I've used it actively as a recruiting, feedback, and development tool—but let me share these ideas with you in this chapter. I have framed them into three groups that I feel are critical to leading large organizations and big change programs.

## A. Building an Agenda

The first skill required for great leadership is *pattern recognition*. In essence, this is the ability to see underlying relationships and get at the meaning beneath the surface. Leaders with this skill can distinguish the important factors in a situation from the noise, demonstrate this insight to their colleagues through discussions and decisions, and craft a compelling story of the organization's challenges and opportunities.

The ability to sit back and watch the horizon instead of concentrating on the hood ornament will keep you going in the right direction. The faster the speed and the more winding the road, the more this principle is true. However, the demands of a business executive require you to also pay attention to the fly on the windshield.

In truth, *both* perspectives are important. You need to narrow the aperture and broaden it at the same time. I know that this is a contradiction, but it can and must be managed. For example, a complete executive leader needs to make sure he is in the details enough to deliver on the current quarter's financials, customer commitments, and projects. Those activities are table stakes. However, you simultaneously need to participate in setting the course for future financials, products and services, human resource needs, and more.

So where should leaders focus their energy? On the immediate crisis: handling this month's budget cuts or projects that have everyone screaming? Or on the longer-horizon issue: the time-consuming analysis of marketplace and technological change?

Good executives are usually good at focusing on one perspective or the other. Great executives are good at both. Leaders must surround themselves with people and partners who can help focus in on complex operating problems and then zoom out to connect the dots. Successful executives are able to assemble a team that can help them spend a reasonable amount of time at both ends of the telescope. In the end, the leader is responsible for not just executing well but that what is being done is the right and valuable stuff.

Another important skill for leadership is *street smarts*. Leaders need to learn who the important players are in their organizations and industries and know what issues matter to them. Leaders must know their organization's history and all the baggage that has built up over time. They have to be politically adept, leveraging their relationships with people to address problems and opportunities.

Street smarts are pattern recognition, but specifically pattern recognition focused on people and organizations. You have to understand how decisions get made—who the influencers, the experts, and the blockers are—and who will tell you what you want to hear versus what you need to know.

Make no mistake: You can have the widest-aperture vision with great business and technical insights, but if you fail to understand the organization as a whole, you will never sell or implement your agenda.

Having the group work with you rather than against you is what I mean by street smarts. You can rely on the formal power of your position from time to time, but it's much more effective to use your influencing skills. Great leaders don't spend all of their time with the executive team and their direct reports. They get out to front-line workers, go on sales calls, walk the administrative office hallways, warehouses, and manufacturing plants. At Frito-Lay, for example, every year each leader rode a sales route for an entire week. This knowledge and the relationships you build over time are what help to create street smarts.

For example, one of my route rides was in rural East Texas. I got up at 3:00 A.M., drove to the distribution center, and jumped on my assigned route at 5:00 A.M. Other than being physically weary, I was mentally alert and up for my adventure. We called on a number of truck stops, bars, and small grocery stores. I remember a number of things from this experience. First, our route salesman really worked hard; second, he had a great relationship and camaraderie with the proprietors he served; and third, he had a tremendous amount of stale returns.

When I questioned him on his well-above-average-return problem, he explained that all of his problems were in the "lite snack, good for you" line items. He had zero returns on pork rinds, Fritos, or Doritos. I remember him saying "Look around, do you see anyone in this truck stop that is yearning for lite popcorn with their coffee, Pepsi, or beer?"

My next question was "If you know that, why do you keep replenishing items that don't move in these outlets?" He looked at me and said, "Because you guys in Plano Headquarters don't listen. Each brand manager pushes their brand as opposed to what my customers want to buy." Those patterns that I picked up on the streets made me a better systems executive and drove a lot of change.

To set a realistic agenda, leaders also need to be *technically savvy*— able to sort complex issues independently and take advantage of organizational, business and technological opportunities while avoiding fads. Great leaders are also thought leaders. Technical knowledge is often dismissed these days as something leaders can delegate. With everything changing so quickly, it is critical that leaders don't completely delegate technical knowledge to others, but instead stay abreast of important technologies and business trends themselves.

To develop effective pattern recognition skills, you have to remain technically competent. For the past few decades, companies have reversed their thinking about the type of leaders they want to hire. Recruiters have gone from looking for people who have strong technical skills with limited business acumen, to seeking people with strong business skills with limited technical acumen. The trade off that's assumed in this trend is problematic and unnecessary—it assumes you can only have one without the other. This is a mistake. In both business and technology, there are long-range patterns that must be recognized, assimilated, and articulated. But at the same time, significant details must be understood and managed. An effective leader must be skilled in both of these areas.

Being technically savvy doesn't mean that you have to be the best technician in your organization. For most leaders, that would be impossible. What you need is an understanding of the basics— to know what's real and what's marketing, what's hard and what's easy, and what's here now and what's not. You also have to know enough to know who (on your staff or in the marketplace) knows the topics versus who knows the words and slogans.

## B. Building a Foundation

Having set the agenda, you have to sell your ideas and have the credibility that you can pull it off. Over the years, I have debated with management-development professionals about the difference between skills, competencies, qualities, and other such labels. My reaction has been to not care so much about classifications, but to instead focus on describing what a leader is and why leadership is critical.

Character has been the most elusive—it's hard to explain, but you know it when it is there. Leaders must show personal *character*. This means doing and saying what's right, not just what is expedient or what others want to hear—even if it's at substantial personal risk.

Character has been described variously as ethical behavior, intellectual integrity, openness, and honesty. These terms have come to the forefront over the past few years—the attention spawned by corporate excesses. Although Sarbanes-Oxley, corporate governance, and ethical guidelines are top of mind these days, they are simply table stakes. You can't run a modern corporation in this country without them.

My definition of character was formed as a young man by role models—not rules and regulations. It is what you do, not what you say. I've worked for and with many terrific leaders over the years in all sorts of corporate cultures. Some of these leaders were collaborative and others were directive, some were relaxed and others intense, and some had command presence while others were quiet and even shy.

I had trouble identifying why I was attracted to so many diverse leadership styles. In my quest for a real role model, it became clear to me that style had little to do with it. The common ingredient that each of these leaders possessed was the substance of their character. No matter what the issue or the struggle or the possible personal gain or loss, they always—not just occasionally—did the right thing. And not only the right thing from a business or economic perspective, but the right thing including the social and philosophical dimensions.

This consistency of character is hard to describe but easy to recognize. People will rally around leaders who do the right things consistently. They know they can count on their leaders to be open and honest at every fork in the road and to take a stand—regardless of the personal risk. When people feel their leaders are erratic, political, or detached from them, they will become cynical. They may do their work but they won't be committed. Trust can only be built over time, so do not become discouraged if people take a show-me attitude.

Given a leader that people will follow is foundational. However, great execution requires *building a great team*. Leaders need committed people to be successful. Building a great team requires mastery both of hard management skills (such as establishing clear performance expectations and dealing firmly with poor performers) and soft skills (such as mentoring and celebrating team successes). It requires investing a lot of time in the development of your people. Leaders must foster passion among their staffs and suppliers and build a sense of enthusiasm for the work at hand.

Organizations are seldom led by a single person, no matter how charismatic he or she may be. The team at the top determines the environment and the culture. The team decides what gets rewarded, punished, recognized, and ignored. Although they do not run all of the plays, it's their job to call them. For leaders, it's important to remember that the team at the top represents and reflects your own true character and agenda. Regardless of what you say you believe, who you choose for your IT leadership team speaks much more loudly. So choosing and developing your leadership team is the single most important competency of a leader. This is a time-consuming task. Many great leaders talk about spending up to one-third of their time on leadership development.

When I was at PepsiCo, developing others was a major part of the life of an executive. The role models were plentiful, leadership competencies were well-known, feedback was continuous, and growth was expected—and often achieved. Unfortunately, most leaders deliver feedback only once a year—most often in a performance evaluation—rather than conducting an ongoing structured development effort. I encourage you, as a leader, to make the investment in sustained leadership development for your IT organization. It will pay tremendous dividends and help give you and your organization leverage and continuity.

The final leadership skill within this category is *influence and persuasion*. I am convinced that in the next few years, the importance of influence and persuasion skills for leaders will only grow. Leading other executives and front-line workers to a full understanding of the game-changing nature of WHY and WHAT will require a planned approach to influencing. Involving others in decisions to get their opinions and buy in, and customizing your approach for each group is critical. There are limits to your personal power, no matter where you sit in the hierarchy. Only by persuading others to support your course can you move the organization in the right direction on a sustained basis.

CEOs, CFOs, CIOs, and other executives have inherent positional power. Soon after I became CIO at Frito-Lay, I would sometimes make an off-the-cuff remark about the organization without much thought. The next thing I knew, people were actually beginning to execute on one of those remarks, or worse, I had hurt someone with an offhand comment. I began to realize just how much weight my positional power carried.

Executives tend to think it is much easier and less time consuming to just tell their direct reports what to do. Part of leadership, however, lies in spending time to explain a direction, in giving employees perspective, and in helping them understand the WHY behind the direction. This is influence, the flip side of positional power. It is easy to rely on positional power and forget the usefulness of influencing skills.

Influencing and selling your ideas are subtly different skills. In selling there's a presumption that you have all the answers, and you set out to persuade everyone else. But in influencing, a great leader will create an involvement with his or her staff and a dialogue on decision making because the door swings both ways. It's possible that you are wrong and your managers have a better idea. Understand, however, that an open dialogue doesn't relieve you of the leadership responsibility to make a decision and move the team forward.

## C. Having an Impact

All of the above—building the agenda and the foundation— are critical pregame activities because the goal of every leader should be to have an impact. However, even teams with great skills and high levels of dedication can fail to have an impact because of their inability to form successful partnerships with their stakeholders, act decisively, or stay focused. I have gathered together a few examples from my career in which these competencies made the difference for me and my teams and left a lasting impact on those organizations.

A lot of lip service is paid today to the notion that leaders should act as great *business partners*. It has become vitally important that leaders fully engage with their colleagues in the business— not simply to get their buy in on projects, but to provide input that business leaders actively seek out. They need to articulate unstated business needs and guide the organization to better processes and solutions, tactfully challenging their colleagues' positions when necessary.

When I was CIO at Frito-Lay in the mid-1980s, we deployed handheld computers for 10,000 route salesmen. Executing this project required establishing and maintaining close partnerships with route drivers, hardware vendors, software providers, telecommunications companies, and customers. Twenty-five years ago, mobile technology was still largely a dream. This was particularly true in a rugged environment like a route truck. Temperatures of 120 degrees in the Southwest and 30 below zero in the upper Midwest could melt and freeze the ink in the printers. In order to ensure that the solution worked in extreme weather conditions, we focused on two model divisions—one in Texas and the other in Minnesota.

Because most of the technology was being integrated for the first time under these conditions, many vendors needed to participate. The IT department acted as a general contractor—coordinating the vendors with Frito-Lay salespeople, managers, and our customers. We had to make vendors our partners and inspire them to stay with the project when it seemed like it was more trouble than it was worth.

The motivation for the project was that servicing customers had become extremely complex. The paperwork that the customer and the salesperson had to deal with was time consuming and often full of errors. It was so cumbersome that salespeople frequently had to finish this paperwork at night—at their kitchen tables.

To provide the team with a vision of the future, we produced an eight-minute film with William Shatner, reenacting these cumbersome tasks and demonstrating how business would be improved if we got the project done. The theme was enterprise and adventure and "Captain Kirk" was the narrator. Once we deployed a few systems, we added to the film testimonials from the salespeople who were using them and showed the film again. When other salespeople heard the feedback from their peers, it cemented their stake in the project. We engaged our technology providers as partners by deemphasizing organizational differences between them and my IT team. People didn't necessarily know or care whether their coworkers on the project were employed by Frito-Lay or one of our suppliers.

My Frito-Lay business leader on the sales operations side was Ron Rittenmeyer. Ron's job was to assemble a team of high-performing people that would work seamlessly with the developers and thousands of route salesmen and our customers. In the end, thousands of people contributed to this effort. My job was to partner with Ron and create this phenomenal force all moving in the same direction.

Once you've gained an understanding of WHY, WHAT, and HOW and have built your team, you're ready to make a difference. Leaders need to have a high profile in their organizations— they must set a course for others to follow toward strategically important goals. They must act with *bold decisiveness*—when there's a difficult decision to be made, they don't hesitate. You know you've become an impact player when you can accomplish tasks without having to always lean on your formal authority. The credibility you've built gives weight to your opinions.

When I was at Delta Air Lines in the late 1990s, my team and I were able to have an impact on the company's business processes by acting decisively to address Delta's Y2K problem. Before my arrival in 1998, Delta had done a lot of design work around what was called the Airport of the Future. The intent was to make travel more enjoyable by providing better information to passengers and cutting down the time they spent waiting in lines.

For example, customers were frustrated because they believed that Delta reservations agents were lying to them about flight information. The actual reason was because different agents using different systems had conflicting data. The gate agents were a major part of the Delta experience and they were frustrated because they couldn't serve their customers effectively.

Over several years, the company had attempted to improve the customer experience, but these attempts were never sustained. I was brought in mainly because Delta had a huge Y2K problem: 60 million lines of code on 30 technology platforms. Within a couple of months, our choice became clear. We could spend the next two years remediating all of the airport systems, or we could bulldoze them and replace them with new technology and processes. Based on our knowledge of the systems, we were confident that replacing them was the best choice. We presented our conclusion to the Delta executive committee and board of directors. With very little time to act, then-CEO Leo Mullin agreed with our recommendation that we should devote our energy to replacement instead of remediation. Once this decision was made, it generated positive energy and dedication from the IT organization and the airport personnel to getting the job done. There was no going back, and everyone knew it.

However, once you've set a course, leaders need to be *resilient and solutions oriented*. When there are problems—as there inevitably are—leaders will need to emphasize solutions rather than hurdles. When you are engaged in game-changing initiatives, you're the one who needs to develop new approaches to work over, around, and through obstacles and setbacks. No matter how—or how much—you plan, in the end most great things are accomplished by resilient organizations.

My experience at Burlington Northern Santa Fe taught me the most about the importance of being resilient and staying focused. I was CIO at Burlington Northern in September 1995 when the merger with Santa Fe was announced. We decided to combine our systems, processes and facilities, and become one railroad in 24 months. This decision did not allow much time to lay out our combined IT infrastructure and integrated application plan. Since we took only 90 days to make the decision on which systems from which railroad would survive, we faced a never-ending stream of surprises and crises that threatened to derail us.

We were constantly frustrated by technical problems we had not planned for, and we needed to keep improvising. To keep the teams focused and optimistic, I took them to see *Apollo 13*—the film about the aborted 1970 moon mission that required the rescue of three astronauts—which was playing in a theater in Ft. Worth. The story reinforced my belief that great things are accomplished by great people working together and never giving up. But it also brought us back to reality. NASA and the astronauts were dealing with life and death—we were merely dealing with a railroad merger. We finished the integration three months early because we stayed focused on what we had signed up to achieve.

Even though Frito-Lay, Delta Air Lines, and the BNSF merger were three of the largest and highest risk business/ technology programs and the work was brutal, almost everyone involved would look back with pride and a sense of great accomplishment.

## WHO Principle III: Culture Matters

That leads me to a discussion of why organization *culture matters*. Many people believe that the subject of culture is a very soft concept and hard to describe. I find that it is the opposite—a very real concept that is easy to describe. It is the mortar that makes bricks (or the building blocks) into a strong and durable wall.

In his book *On Leadership*, John Gardner talks about the release of human possibilities:

> Many factors contribute to the rise of civilization—accidents of resource availability, geographical considerations, preeminence in trade or military power and so on. But whatever the other ingredients, a civilization rises to greatness when something happens in human minds... At the heart of sustained morale and motivation lie two ingredients that appear somewhat contradictory: on the one hand, positive attitudes toward the future and toward what one can accomplish through one's own intentional acts, and on the other hand, recognition that life is not easy and that nothing is ever finally safe.[8]

A high-performing team needs trust, hope, enjoyment, and opportunity.

---

[8] On Leadership by John Gardner

## Trust

The need for trust in your staff is a given. You cultivate trust by setting boundaries within which people have certain freedoms (to make decisions, to take risks, to speak their minds) as well as certain obligations (to speak the truth, to be accountable for their decisions, to learn from their mistakes). People can't be productive when they are driven only by rules, nor can anything be achieved when there are no boundaries and chaos reigns.

I've seen cultures at both extremes over the years. In one company where I worked, there were rules for everything and bureaucracy dominated the management system. The environment was orderly, but there was almost no room for individual judgment, and therefore, no one felt any ownership of their work or motivation to do it quickly. At the other extreme, I worked for a company that was so decentralized it was chaotic. Every group made up its own rules as it saw fit.

Neither of these environments led to high performance. But in a framework where people are trusted to operate, people will give their best. I have gone into environments where teams within the IT department were so rigidly organized that one group was unwilling to share its expertise with another. When we reorganized, my direct reports agreed to be evaluated on how well they shared their staffs with each other. They stopped hoarding talent and started trusting each other. Employees became more productive, and quality went up.

## Hope

It is important to understand that high-performing people have dreams for achievement that need to be fueled by hope. It's a truism that people will flourish when they have hope, and that they give up and become despondent when hope subsides. High performers thrive on the recognition they get from working through hard issues and persevering. This perseverance requires optimism. The job of a leader in a hopeful environment is to be realistic and optimistic at the same time. Realism acknowledges the facts of a situation—no matter how unpleasant—while optimism dictates that given the facts, we continue to work toward our goals. When confronted with a team that has lost hope, it is critical to acknowledge the facts and then begin to generate ideas for how to solve our problems. The notion that "life is lousy and then you die" is not an acceptable leadership quality. There are very few things that cannot be solved if you can keep hope alive.

## Enjoyment

Make the work environment enjoyable. People perform at peak levels when they enjoy what they do and with whom they do it. Don't confuse enjoyment with frivolity, however, or with the absence of challenging work. Real enjoyment at work comes when you and your team are deeply immersed in tackling a problem, and you persevere and succeed together. You can be intense and relaxed at the same time if you are confident in yourself and those around you. Just as you can sense this tension in athletes when the game is on the line, you can sense it in a leader. When you communicate that combination of competitive fire and inner peace, you communicate to your team that, if we give everything we have, support each other, and persevere, we will succeed.

You can set the tone that work is fun by demonstrating that you enjoy your job, that you like your staff, and that you appreciate how hard they work. Sometimes, this is as simple as saying thank you to someone who worked all weekend. If you can laugh at mistakes instead of blaming people for them, your team can focus on winning instead of not failing. If someone is working 60 hours a week, you should not care if he takes a two-hour lunch. But no one can sustain 60-hour weeks and be a healthy, vibrant human being. Something is wrong if that becomes a way of life.

## Opportunity

The last challenge is to create an environment in which people can grow. Top performers need to learn new skills and develop new ideas in order to work at their peak. People who learn new things, work with diverse groups of people, and are given the opportunity to experience different roles that expand their worldview produce a richer organization. These skills and perspective-building mechanisms help to create people who respect differences, are more self-assured, who listen well, and are more curious. This is different than the step-by-step process of acquiring skills that we know, but it's necessary because the rate and scope of change have increased so dramatically.

It is important to rotate people through different parts of the business. One of the mechanisms we used was actually called a "Move Meeting." Every three weeks each of my directors would come to a meeting with a list of staffing needs for their projects, and a list of people available to move over the next one-to-three months. Our goal was to fill important jobs with our best talent. Since our calibration pointed out the talent levels of every individual, there was no ability to hide good talent or pass off weak players. We also had a guideline that top players could be protected in a position only for 18 months. After that, they would be the organization's to move at will.

This combined with the recruiting process and calibration kept the opportunities alive for our best talent and exposed our low performers. This strategy keeps people energized and motivated to perform at higher levels. It is also critical to move out low performers to create opportunity for high performers.

As a leader, you have the power to influence people and therefore their performance. If you believe in creating an environment where trust, optimism, enjoyment, and personal growth are encouraged, then you will build a sustainable, high-performing team—and, in the process, create many new leaders.

## WHO Principle IV: Performance Matters

The greatest asset any organization has is the talent, commitment, and energy of the people who work each day to produce its products or services. How that talent, commitment, and energy is directed and developed is a key indicator of long-term organizational success.

Managing the performance of an organization is both an art and a science. The science of the performance management system presented here encompasses a systematic approach to performance, development, and succession planning, as well as methods for evaluating and rewarding performance outcomes. The art of engaging people to perform to their optimum ability is much more complex. It entails creating an organizational climate where people thrive and passion for the work is ignited. Central to this idea is an understanding of what motivates and rewards the human spirit.

Don't confuse a performance-management system with a performance-appraisal system. Appraisals are an event. A management system is a way of life with many components. All are extremely time consuming, but when executed together you will get extraordinary results from ordinary people. The six critical components that follow are at the heart of the heralded leadership machines of companies like PepsiCo and General Electric.

**Line organizations own the performance-management process.** Business-unit management is ultimately responsible for the overall performance of an organization. As such, line organizations are the primary owners of the performance-management system. Staff organizations such as human resources serve an important support role as they partner with line management to develop, implement, and continuously improve the performance-management process. But there should be no doubt that the line managers own this process.

**Both managers and employees play a critical role in improving organizational performance.** Leadership and employees must work together to consistently improve individual and organizational performance. While leadership must be able to effectively manage the skills and ignite the passions and energy of people in a way that openly values and rewards their contributions, each individual is responsible for performing to the best of their ability and for increasing their contributions over time.

**Performance must be measured on two dimensions: performance objectives and demonstration of competencies/ values.** Performance is not only determined by what we accomplish, but also by how we accomplish it. Measuring business results against written performance objectives speaks to what we have accomplished. Competency mastery—the ability to demonstrate the thinking, planning, and relationship skills that allow us to work together in an efficient, effective, and productive manner—provides a second, and equally important, measure of performance. Demonstration of the values of the organization is often included in the competency dimension.

**Performance contributions must be differentiated across like jobs.** For the performance bar to be raised across an organization in a meaningful way, exceptional performance needs to be recognized and rewarded differently than solid performance, and solid performance differently than poor performance. In addition to each manager being able to differentiate among members of their own workgroup, it is critical that performance be calibrated across workgroups. This assures that expectations and accomplishments for like jobs are viewed consistently across the organization and that several members of management have the opportunity to provide feedback for each individual under review.

**Performance contributions must be tied directly to compensation.** In a pay-for-performance system, performance levels are rewarded differently. Compensation in the form of incentive pay and merit increases vary depending on overall contribution levels.

**Performance improvement requires feedback, coaching, and developmental opportunities.** A primary responsibility of leadership is to coach the development of others. In addition to formal performance management activities, great leaders continuously seek to use teachable moments—naturally occurring opportunities to provide performance feedback and coaching. Coaching improvement or reinforcing desired performance close to the time of the event ensures learning and aids in relationship building.

Providing employees with regular feedback about their performance is one of the most important activities a manager can do. Feedback should not be limited to the time of formal evaluation periods nor given only when an employee has made a mistake. Finding informal opportunities to praise good work, as well as to coach development, is critical to building a high-performance organization.

The four principles that matter—Organization, Leadership, Culture, and Performance—are critical to successful, IT-enabled business transformation. As I indicated earlier in this chapter, most organizations are 100–200 leaders throughout their enterprises away from being able to pull off this type of large-scale change. Companies will spend hundreds of millions—if not billions—of dollars over time, and in an increasing number of cases they will be betting their future on these investments. It is, therefore, critical to have the right people in the right positions throughout the organization who can share the vision and work through the issues.

This was the case at Frito-Lay, Delta Air Lines, and BNSF. Granted, we had a clear mission, a compressed timeframe, the money, and full support of the executive team. However, during the journey our issues and problems were far larger and more numerous than we could have anticipated. It was the leadership culture from top to bottom that held each of us accountable to one another, replaced excuses with solutions, and supported and encouraged rather than criticized and punished.

In the next—and final—chapter of this book, I will summarize the framework into a condensed model for you to use as your own personal reference guide to IT-enabled change.

# CHAPTER 7

## Now It's Your Turn

# 7 NOW IT'S YOUR TURN

Over the years, I have scanned many business books and was able to pick up an idea or two from each and make some use of them. This book is somewhat different in its makeup because I have presented a system, not a set of isolated ideas. Leave out or minimize any part of the system and the results will be severely limited.

To get world-class results over time requires that members of the executive team play their positions well and embrace a systemic approach to IT-enabled change and business-systems modernization. To achieve this kind of modernization, the business leadership needs to engage with the CIO—and engage early—because both understanding the business requirements and what technology can make possible is essential to success.

In enterprises that do this well, the CIO is more than a Chief Information Officer, he or she is a Chief Integration Officer because managing across boundaries and understanding the systems possibilities and limits of technology are required to bring about a seamless, flexible enterprise. The CIO must envision the system that is the enterprise. Sorting through the complexity of this dialogue can be simplified and the blind spot can be eliminated if the combined leadership team focuses on the following questions for the enterprise:

- How do customers want to transact business?
- What is the value of supply-chain leverage?
- What are the givens for our industry?
- How quickly are our customers moving to a different set of demands?
- How quickly are our competitors moving to fill their demands?
- Are there new entrants to the competitive scene?
- In a multi-divisional company, what gives us synergy versus what gives us autonomy? How and where are these decisions made?
- How can the transformation occur, and how can we keep the business stable during the necessary changes?
- How can we leverage the existing talent, skills, and expertise that will be required to keep the existing systems healthy and also build toward the future target?
- How can we improve the probability of success and minimize the risks typically associated with changes of this magnitude?
- What should the pacing of investments be, both short term and long term?

As we begin to answer these practical questions, our approach will become business led and the executive committee can take part in this common-sense dialogue.

The way the CIO enters this dialogue sets the stage for the quality and efficiency of the IT component. If the strategic dialogue is entered early and proactively—and without jargon—then the proper give and take can be put on the problem. If it is entered passively—by trying to service each function head's tactical view—then the end result will be poorly constructed, disconnected projects. It will be difficult to extract the business value from such a result, and nearly impossible to justify. The other trap is to create a grand vision and then to attempt to build it in one massive greenfield program.

As I wrap up, I think it would be helpful to review the components and reinforce the roles and accountability of leadership along each part of the journey. The first and most critical steps belong to the CEO and his entire team. Sustainable change happens only when there is a compelling reason to change and a call to arms. I have witnessed many change programs that fell short because they came from the middle of the enterprise and not the top. They were focused only on the current problems, were narrow in scope, were not well articulated, or were not that critical.

The term "strategic plan" has been overused and abused and has become somewhat academic in a world that is both tumultuous and that requires short-term navigation. Being part of executive committees in the 1980s gave us time to think and plan the future. By 2008, an executive committee meeting was like going through the rapids of a swift-and-unpredictable river. One problem after another, new customer demands, a kaleidoscope of new competitors, economic threats, government interventions, and phenomenal quarter-to-quarter pressure to perform abounded.

So what replaces strategy? How can an executive team address the future while keeping an eye on the road immediately ahead of them? What are the main ingredients of a 21st century WHY change and WHAT to change model?

The answers to these questions differ by company and industry, but the common threads are flexibility, speed, low cost, value creation, responsiveness, and innovation. The important point is that although you cannot be precise about the future, you can determine patterns and be limber enough to continuously move forward and be within striking distance of performing well as new dynamics present themselves.

Becoming less fixed and more variable is a cornerstone of flexibility. Serving customers the way they want to transact business will be table stakes. Doing it without destroying your economics, leverage, and quality will require clever system design and product innovation. As the executive team imagines the future, it is critical to not be constrained by your current business model. Do not be limited by how hard or expensive it might be or how long it will take. Be intentionally unrealistic in this phase, and think outside your normal limits—the constraints of the system can and should be articulated during the HOW and WHO phases.

After you have framed the WHY and WHAT storyline, you should begin to engage the next level of leadership and selected frontline people to begin to formulate the HOW. The simple question is this: If we were going to change the enterprise over time, how would we go about it? To go about this work would require your team to grasp the compelling vision of the future, combined with the belief that without changing course and speed you are all on a burning platform. This is easier to do if you really are in trouble. However, by then, your resources are probably already limited.

The healthier approach is to be able to describe a future burning platform that will exist if the organization does not alter its current course. That takes a lot more internal selling. Try to get your most articulate and trusted leaders out in front and passionate about the opportunities of achieving the vision.

This is where the CIO and the IT organization need to step up and articulate what is possible from both a business-systems and technology vantage point. Building the future blueprints for business processes, application workflows, information architecture, user experience, and security are all part of the artifacts that will be required before anyone begins to modernize the enterprise. They must work closely with the operating teams as they articulate how sales, marketing, operations, supply chain, finance, and human resources need to change the way they will operate, measure, and compensate performance in the future state. In fact, it is the intersection of business architecture and IT architecture that will create the flexibility that we saw in the Frito-Lay journey.

Once the future state is envisioned and the current state is described, you have the load-bearing pillars you need to begin laying out the gap-closing plan. This is where the constraints begin to shape the journey. How long will it take? How much will it cost? What is the sequencing? What are the practical changes I can make to my capital assets like a plant, equipment, fleet, and my human resources by country, law, unions, severance, and more?

Moving early—before you have a crisis—is harder to articulate but easier to traverse. Once you have set your course, assuming you have time to make the changes you need to make, it really does not matter if it takes you five years or ten years. You will be amazed at how much progress can be made in just two to four years, given the latitude and longitude of a new destination. This is particularly true for the IT components. The physical assets and operations will take longer to reconfigure.

Finally, we get to the WHO. This will not happen without talented and committed leaders and frontline people. Competing for talent has been the strength of some organizations and the Achilles heel of others. World-class enterprises have world-class talent-management systems that focus on constantly upgrading their human resources. They both recruit well and develop their internal people well. The vibrancy of these organizations is palpable regardless of the economic downturns or booms. Talented leaders are always the limiting factor to success. In bad times they have the resilience to play through, and the personality and credibility to inspire the people around them. In good times they make up a bench that can fill leadership positions that growth creates. Focus on this dimension of change before you spend much money on the others.

## Always On

We have now evolved to a 21st century, information-intensive, always-on model of commerce. This new era of global commerce and connectivity make the intersection of IT and business invariably intertwined. It used to be good enough to be either operationally excellent or customer centric or innovative. Now all three—or at least two out of the three—are table stakes and all need to be technology enabled, or at least supported.

This has been underscored over the last year. The economic downturn has pressurized most enterprises to where small inefficiencies and customer-service cracks have become significant. As the tide has lowered, what looked like calm seas to many organizations are now exposed as rocks beneath the waterline. When the economy recovers, revenue may cover the problems. But make no mistake, the structural issues will remain. Most successful 20th century companies need to aggressively rethink and retool for a new era. Most enterprises must begin to think about the subject of technology-enabled business change, or they will fail to be competitive and eventually even to exist.

I believe that this framework can help build the bridge between business leaders who have a blind spot and do not understand IT, and IT leaders who struggle with business issues. I have seen it work for myself, in many different industries, and with many different leaders and teams. As I said earlier in the book, it is now time—after 50 years of IT—to manage this profession in a more structured and understandable way. I hope that my own 40 years of travelling down a hard road will contribute to your endeavors.

## ACKNOWLEDGMENTS

IT is a very young profession compared to manufacturing, engineering, sales, accounting, etc. I joined this profession in the mid 1960s, when IT was in its infancy. Over the last 45 years, we have developed an extraordinary body of knowledge that can be shared by the entire leadership community of business and IT. Unfortunately, like anything else, much of the learning has been by trial and error.

Over the decades, I have made my share of mistakes but I was always surrounded by highly talented people. Through their optimism, skill, and commitment we kept improving on the framework that is the core to this book and that will help eliminate IT as a blind spot. This book is a tribute to the men and women of Frito-Lay, Burlington Northern Santa Fe, Coors Brewing Company, Coca-Cola, FedEx, Southwest Airlines and the many other clients we worked with over the years...

First Data, Delta Air Lines, The Home Depot, Oshawa Group, AmeriServe Food Distribution, PriceWaterhouseCoopers (PwC), Manpower, WellPoint, Interliant, Kemper Insurance, ERCOT, Agilent, MBNA, Westinghouse/CBS, Interpublic Group of Companies (IPG), PepsiCo, Agora Foods, Payless Shoes, Heidrick & Struggles, Bank of America, State of Illinois, Norfolk Southern, Royal Bank of Canada, Green Mountain, EDS, BMC, Pier 1 Imports, e.Original, Hewlett-Packard, Luminant Worldwide, McKinsey & Company, Universal Studios, NPULSE, Boeing, Fluor Corp, A G Edwards Technology Group, PowerUp Networks, EYT, LATIS, Prosavvy, MyExpressLane.com, Mashantucket Pequot Tribal Nation, Dell, American Express Financial Advisors, Bluefire Systems, Fingerhut, NGC and Gold Systems.

In particular, I'd like to acknowledge all of the tremendously talented people that ventured out with me to form and build The Feld Group. It is from their hard work and dedication that this framework for IT-enabled business transformation was honed from 1992-2003. These were the best of the best — and we made each other better.

Raji Abraham, Vince Accardo, Stan Alexander, Dawn Allred, Andrew Arroyo, John Ashman, Becky Beggs, Tony Bianco, Matt Bieri, Mark Bilger, Chris Bird, Brian Bissell, Anita Brown, Scott Buhlman, Tim Carroll, Mike Caruso, Dan Cavey, Clint Combs, Karen Cook, Alan Cooper, Deborah Covin, Samantha Crosby, Bryan Crumpton, Rick Davidson, Richard Davis, Ted DellaVecchia, Debbie Deveroux, Bret Dixon, Sid Dobias, Bob Ebersole, Kenny Feld, Tony Ferrendelli, Tony Ferri, Kris Fitzgerald, Ed Flaherty, Dan Greer, Bruce Graham, Keith Halbert, Anita Hale, Joe Hanson, Sandy Hawk, Mike Herskovitz, Janita Herrin, Dexter Herring, Brian Hickey, Janice Hoyt, Mark Jankowski, JR Jesson, Jan Johnson, Amy Jones, Monte Jones, John Karnes, Blair Koch, Rick Kochhar, Mike Koehler, Suresh Krishnan, Mark Kuane, Don Mann, Jan Marshall, Luis Martin, Joe McCartin, Chris McClelen, Brent McClintock, Jim McCrory, Tom Merritt, Michael Moffitt, Sam Moultrie, Tom Nealon, Dave Newman, Drew Newman, Ajay Nuna, Gloria Olive, Birken Olson, Sara Osterhaus, Toby Pennycuff, Lalo Perez, Lisa Prassack, Arun Rao, Jeff Redman, John Reeves, Doug Register, Ed Robben, Subodh Samuel, Roger Salter, Mike Sanders, Steve Schuckenbrock, Mitch Seagraves, Scott Shafer, Janine Shelby, Jackie Shelton, Siva Sivakumaran, Tim Smith, Jason Spears, Pat Steele, Rob Stockwell, Brad Taylor, Rich Thompson, Andrew Toback, Steve van Niman, Steve Vaughn, Russell Villemez, Jeff Wade, Becky Walker, Becky Wanta, Tom Wiegmann, Donna Wilson, and Tim Wright.